# Prophetic Masquerade
## Learn to Use the Word of God to Unmask
## the Wolves Among the Sheep

# Prophetic Masquerade
## Learn to Use the Word of God to Unmask the Wolves Among the Sheep

by
# Kevin R. Kleint

*Dedicated to:*

My amazing wife and three beautiful children ...
this book is a testimony to your trials and sufferings as much
as it is a testimony to mine.  You are my treasure.


and to


My mother ...
Your prayers were not in vain.


and (last but not least)


*My wonderful editors*
*who worked very hard to make this a quality work ....*

# Table of Contents

# INTRODUCTION

*"Kevin, you may not be a false prophet, but you're contributing to his ministry, so you will share the same punishment."*

Those painful words spoken by a friend echoed through my head as I stepped out into the parking lot. I had just completed my final day as the webmaster for (arguably) the most popular prophetic web ministry of the 00's. A mix of emotions washed over me. Relief... sorrow... and most of all... regret.

For seven years, I was unable to be a caring father to my little children and a strong, godly husband to my wife. I had verbally and emotionally abused my family, putting them through the ringer because I was so stressed and angry.

For seven years, I had worked for a ministry/business under the delusion that I was helping people, when I was actually contributing to their demise.

For seven years, I watched as this ministry grew from 30,000 subscribers and around 10 employees to over 130,000 subscribers and around 50 employees.

I watched the money come in. I saw the corruption.

And I held a lot of guilt.

I realized that I was only obeying orders from my boss, but when the rubber met the road, I was the one who created the emails, I was the one who trimmed the images, I was the one who hit the "Publish" button.

I was the one who distributed false prophecy to the world.

Now, on an international scale, this same false prophetic ministry is viewed by hundreds of thousands as "The Source" to go to if you want to find the latest word from the Creator.

And I contributed to this deception.

As I opened the door to my car, I knew that I would eventually need to do something to make it right, so I embarked on this crazy journey with Jesus, using the Word as my guide.

I spent the *next seven years* studying prophets and prophecy in the Bible from Genesis to Revelation. You can find a lot of information on my web site, http://www.HonorOfKings.org.

This book is the culmination of my studies.

## WHY BE SO CRITICAL OF THE PROPHETIC MOVEMENT?

People often ask me why I am so convinced that the modern day prophetic movement is a false and/or deceptive movement. The simple answer is that there is an overwhelming amount of Scripture to support this viewpoint. If I were to willfully ignore the abundance of scriptural evidence supplied in God's Word (as so many often do), then I would be committing a grievous sin.

Many believers have been taught that discerning a prophet has to be complicated. I don't see it that way. If you compare the words and characteristics of a "prophet" to the Word of God, the matter becomes quite simple. You just have to be willing to accept what the Word of God says is the truth - and that's not always easy to do in today's politically correct, have-it-your-way society.

Approximately 30% of the Word of God is comprised of real prophecies written by men who were true prophets of the Most High. If you add in the multitude of Scriptures scattered throughout the rest of the Bible referencing prophets, prophecies and false prophets, the percentage gets much, much higher.

I believe that God did this intentionally, to assist us in our discernment in these Last Days.

## GOD DOES NOT WANT YOU TO BE DECEIVED

The Messiah told us:

> **Mark 13:22-23 (also see Matthew 24:24)**
> *For false christs and false prophets will rise and show signs and wonders to deceive, if possible, even the elect. But take heed; see, I have told you all things beforehand.*

Believe me, friends, it is not God's will for you to be among those deceived by these false prophets and the clever words they say.

In this book, I will give you an abundance of Scripture that **YOU** can use as a reference to help you discern those who call themselves prophets/prophetesses but are actually deceived, or outright liars. I didn't compose this list with ill-will towards anyone in the modern day prophetic movement. In fact, many people who are caught up in this false movement are genuine, sincere people, who do *"many wonderful works."* Nevertheless, when you compare their words and characteristics to what the Word of God says, they are identical to false prophets.

## THE IMAGE OF A FALSE PROPHET

As you read through this book, seriously consider the Scriptures that I will be highlighting and re-create the image of a false prophet as your mind is being renewed according to the Word. It is vital that you let your man-made doctrines, personal biases and human reasoning submit to the authority of the Word. The wolves among the sheep will become evident when you do so.

The Word says to let a matter be established by *"two or three witnesses."*

By the time you are done reading this book, you will have **at least 10 witnesses from Scripture** to help you test the alleged prophet. You will also have ironclad proof that 99% of the modern-day prophets are not who they claim to be.

I want to stress that it is not the will of God for us to be deceived.

At the same time, it is up to us to do our due diligence and *"study to show ourselves approved."* We are going to dig deep into Scripture and study the characteristics of a false prophet. After you read these chapters, ask yourself,

"Are the 'prophets' I listen to true, or are they false?"

Remember, this is a True/False answer. Contrary to what you may have been taught, there is no "gray area" with God's Word.

## GIVE OTHERS THIS INFORMATION!

Finally, I want to encourage you to give (or loan) this book to your friends after you are done reading it. This book will greatly benefit the following groups of people:

- *Those who question the modern day prophetic movement;*

- *Those who call themselves prophets and/or are involved in the prophetic movement;*

- *Those who are drawn to the "show" of the prophetic movement;*

- *Those who want to stay aligned with the Word and not be deceived in these Final Days.*

If you know anyone that falls into any of these groups, please share this information!

As we approach the end, it is VITAL that we remain on the path laid out for us in His Word.

One mistake can have eternal consequences.

**For the Truth,**

**Kevin Kleint**
**Web Site:** http://www.honorofkings.org
**Email:** kevinkleint@outlook.com

# SCRIPTURAL WITNESS #1: FALSE PROPHETS LOOK LIKE SHEEP

Discerning false prophets can be really difficult for most people, because they are always looking for the "bad guy." They have a mental picture of some perverse, wicked man with glowing slits for eyes and a cruel grin. Maybe it's a woman in heavy make-up dressed in a slinky dress with a sign reading "I am Jezebel" hung around her neck.

This is the **exact opposite** of what a false prophet/prophetess will usually look like.

> ### Matthew 7:15
> *Beware of false prophets, who come to you in sheep's clothing, but inwardly they are ravenous wolves.*

The truth is, false prophets are some of the nicest people you will ever meet!

When I worked for the Elijah List, I had the opportunity to meet several false prophets. With the exception of a few, they were all very warm and caring people. Even to this day, they do not realize that, according to the Word of God, they are false prophets. Their minds simply cannot fathom that their gentle demeanor and *"many wonderful works"* will not be considered when they are judged in that day.

This is both scary and sobering.

Today's wolves have no clue that they are wolves! They each look down at the wool clothes that cover their bodies and they think within themselves "I'm a sheep!" – but inwardly, they are full of covetousness and excess. They only crave their next source of "nourishment."

Jesus said that in that final day, many false prophets would say:

### Matthew 7:22b
*Lord, Lord, have we not prophesied in thy name? and in thy name have cast out devils? and in thy name done many wonderful works?*

We absolutely must comprehend this.

- **Prophesying** in Jesus' name will not ensure you a place in the Kingdom.

- **Casting out devils** in Jesus' name will not ensure you a place in the Kingdom.

- **"Doing the stuff"** (whether that be miracles or acts of kindness) in Jesus' name will not ensure you a place in the Kingdom.

At the End of the Age, false prophets will be a group of people who are clueless to the fact that they walked contrary to His Word and His Will. They will think:

*"I did the works! I healed the sick, cleansed the leper and did many wonderful works - IN JESUS NAME! Surely I'm guaranteed a spot in His Kingdom! He used me to heal!"*

But, according to Scripture, they have a rude awakening coming.

# SCRIPTURAL WITNESS #2: FALSE PROPHETS ALWAYS DRAW A CROWD

If I see a prophet with a large following, red flags go off in my head right away. Usually, when a prophet is surrounded by many people, it is because the people like what they hear.

For the most part, true prophets in the Bible were NOT well-liked by those in authority or the masses because they pointed out sin and tried to steer the listener back to obedience to God's simple commands. Such a message is not well accepted by a carnal society - or the church, for that matter.

Jesus warned us, saying:

> **Luke 6:26**
> *Woe to you when all men speak well of you, <u>for so did their fathers to the false prophets.</u>*

This is a "New Testament Warning" straight from our Messiah's mouth, exhorting the disciple to resist the urge to pander to the crowd. The masses will follow blindly after anyone who will tell them what they want to hear, lavishing upon them esteem and adoration when they should be looking to the One who created them.

But true prophets of the Most High do not need the praise of the people. They look to Him for their acceptance.

## DOES THAT MEAN EVERYONE WHO DRAWS A CROWD IS A FALSE PROPHET?

Not at all! John the Baptist, Jesus and Moses each had quite a following!

So, how do you discern the difference?

Jesus said:

> **Matthew 7:15-16a**
> *Beware of false prophets, who come to you in sheep's clothing, but inwardly they are ravenous wolves. <u>You will know them by their fruits.</u>*

So, what is the fruit of a false prophet? This topic will be explored further in a later chapter. I have also included a teaching of mine entitled *"False Prophets, Fruit and the Unwitting Wolf,"* **[Appendix B]** in the back of this book, where you can read further commentary.

**Meanwhile, remember:** We are looking for *"two or three witnesses"* from Scripture! If you see someone who claims to be a prophet surrounded by a bunch of adoring fans, displaying any of the other "marks" that we will touch on in this book, don't listen to them.

Don't be fearful of speaking out either… you will have your "two or three witnesses" from Scripture. It will be established.

## FALSE PROPHETS HAVE AN INSATIABLE DESIRE FOR STATUS

While studying this principle, I came across something interesting that bears mentioning.

Most of us are familiar with the verse that says *"Satan transforms himself into an angel of light."* Paul wrote this while addressing the issue of false apostles who desired to be regarded and honored in the same way he (Paul) was.

> **2 Corinthians 11:12-14**
>
> *But what I do, I will also continue to do, <u>that I may cut off the opportunity from those who desire an opportunity to be regarded just as we are</u> in the things of which they boast. For such are false apostles, deceitful workers, <u>transforming themselves into apostles of Christ</u>. And no wonder! For Satan himself <u>transforms himself into an angel of light</u>.*

Granted, this is talking about false apostles, but the dynamic is the same for a false prophet (both then and now). The false prophets also desire to be regarded as equal to the prophets of the Bible, all the while preaching *"another Jesus"* (read all of **2 Corinthians 11** for context).

This willingness to teach something other than what the Word really says (preaching "another Jesus"), combined with a desire for regard (honor) is part of what makes them wolves in sheep's clothing.

They are *"transformed"* into something false... a deceitful worker. Selah.

## FALSE PROPHETS REVEL IN THE FAVOR OF THE PEOPLE WHO PROMOTE THEM

As I mentioned in the last post, false prophets are likeable people, and the multitudes eagerly flock to hear them give the latest encouraging word because they have itching ears.

> **2 Timothy 4:3-4**
>
> *For the time will come when they will not endure sound*

*doctrine, but according to their own desires, because they have <u>itching ears</u>, <u>they will heap up for themselves</u> teachers; and they will turn their ears away from the truth, and be turned aside to fables.*

Did you notice how it was the PEOPLE who heaped up false teachers?

On Judgment Day, the deceived will find themselves **complicit** in their own deception. They will not be able to justly accuse the false prophets and say "You deceived us!" because THEY were the ones who promoted, fawned over and worshiped the ones who deceived them.

I've found out (the hard way) that a false prophet's disciples will defend their idolatry with a vengeance, because the "idol" gives them <u>a false sense of security</u> that justifies them in their sin, or at least gives them license to ignore it.

The true prophet, Isaiah, spoke of these people when he said:

### Isaiah 30:8-11
*Now go, write it before them on a tablet, and note it on a scroll, that it may be for time to come, forever and ever:*

*That this is a rebellious people, lying children, <u>children who will not hear the law of the LORD</u>; Who say to the seers, "Do not see," and to the prophets, "<u>Do not prophesy to us right things; speak to us smooth things, prophesy deceits.</u>*

*Get out of the way, turn aside from the path, <u>cause the Holy One of Israel to cease from before us.</u>"*

## FALSE PROPHETS SPEAK SMOOTH THINGS

Most modern day prophets preach a Jesus that you can reach the easy way, and thousands of hungry people (many of them youth) are flocking to them, eager for *anything* to draw them closer to God.

This should be a major red flag to anyone who is truly watching.

I will write more about *positive and encouraging words* in a later chapter. Just know, for now, that the crowds flock to false prophets because of the "smooth things" that they say. They like what they hear. They like to have the "itchy ear" scratched.

When you see the multitudes being gathered together to listen to the newest teaching or latest revelation, remember that Jesus said it would be the FEW who find the NARROW gate into the NARROW way that leads to LIFE.

> **Matthew 7:13-14**
> *Enter by the narrow gate; for wide is the gate and broad is the way that leads to destruction, and there are MANY who go in by it. Because NARROW is the gate and DIFFICULT is the way which leads to LIFE, and there are FEW who find it.*

Do you see the **"MANY?"**

Remember... Jesus said there would be **"FEW!"**

# SCRIPTURAL WITNESS #3: FALSE PROPHETS SPEAK PRESUMPTUOUSLY

## DEFINING A PRESUMPTUOUS PROPHET

If we read the Webster's dictionary definition,[1] we can see that to "presume" means to assume something is true "*in absence of proof to the contrary.*" From the surrounding information, we can also see that this often involves a deed performed with "*unwarrantable boldness*" or "*without right or permission.*"

If we want to know what God says about a "presumptuous prophet," all we have to do is check out the book of Deuteronomy.

### Deuteronomy 18:20-22

*But the prophet who presumes to speak a word in My name, which I have not commanded him to speak, or who speaks in the name of other gods, that prophet shall die.*

*And if you say in your heart, "How shall we know the word which the LORD has not spoken?"*

*When a prophet speaks in the name of the LORD, if the thing does not happen or come to pass, that [is] the thing which the LORD has not spoken; the prophet has spoken it presumptuously [H2087 – zadown]; you shall not be afraid of him.*

The Hebrew word translated as "presumptuously" is the word **"zadown,"**[2] which basically means the same thing as the Webster's definition.[1]

The root word for **"zadown"** is **"zuwd"**[3] meaning to act proudly and rebelliously. This should speak volumes to us about those who presume to speak the Words of the Most High in a haphazard way.

If we combine all of this information from both the Word of God and our own dictionary, we can safely conclude that a presumptuous prophet is a person who boldly speaks a "word from God" that does not come to pass. This "lack-of-fulfillment" nullifies the validity of their claims of hearing from God accurately, and places them in the category of "the rebellious."

## GOING TO GREAT LENGTHS TO AVOID THE PRESUMPTION ACCUSATION

The truth is, our modern-day prophets are actually quite gutless when it comes to speaking a tried and true prophecy. They would much rather feed their listeners with pretty speech (sometimes accompanied by music), and point to some nebulous event that is impossible to track. This spineless tactic gives them an easy out, should the prophecy fail to come to pass.

As long as no one can hold them accountable, that's one less worry for them.

They are also very fond of spiritualizing obvious weather patterns (and other phenomena) for given areas and associating them with Godly intervention.

- *"Alaska is going to have a heavy snow, symbolizing God's desire to forget your sins and see you as righteous!"*

- *"California is going to have an earthquake because God is wanting to shake your foundations and prepare you for the 'New Thing' that He is doing!"*

- *"There is going to be an eruption of God's Love around the cities and islands in the vicinity of the Ring of Fire!"*

- *"The Pacific Northwest is going to experience a heavy rain, as God rains glory down on the region!"*

This kind of dishonest wordplay should alert people that there is a wolf in their midst, but unfortunately, this is not the case. I've found that people are willing to forgive even the most flagrant abuses of the gift of prophecy.

Just as long as their idol remains safely on the shelf, all is well.

Meanwhile, the false prophet continues to avoid the accusation the he/she is speaking presumptuously, and the masses continue to be deceived.

## PROPHECY AND THE TIMING ISSUE

In my research, probably the most used and abused rationalization for a failed prophecy, the "Grandaddy of them all," is what I would call the "timing issue."

- *"How do we know that what is prophesied will not come to pass later?"*

- *"The Old Testament prophets prophesied many things that didn't come to pass until after they were long gone!"*

- *"There are still MANY end time prophecies that have yet to be fulfilled!"*

False prophets (and the people who love to defend them) will use this rebuttal whenever they want to put the "BIG SMACK DOWN" on anyone who dares to challenge their failed prophecies.

This is usually the "go-to" argument that they use to keep the sheeple in check and their prophetic idols safely resting on their altars.

I will not take an extreme stance on this excuse, because it is valid to a certain degree, but I will offer the following suggestions.

When being confronted with the timing issue, ask yourself the following:

- *Does the overall prophecy lead you back to the commandments of God?*

- *Are the majority of the prophet's prophecies nebulous or unfulfilled yet?*

- *Does the majority of the prophet's prophecies provide him/her an "easy out," like we discussed above?*

- *Does he/she hold any other telltale signs of being a false prophet that I will share in this book?*

While it is true that many prophecies did not come to pass until after the deaths of the biblical prophets, it is also true that these prophets did not fit into any of the other 9 criteria listed here.

Remember, if you have "two or three witnesses," you have yourself a false prophet. It doesn't matter if they are the sweetest people around. It doesn't matter how convincing they are. If they look like false prophets and act like a false prophets, they are not true prophets of the Most High!

## THE TIMING ISSUE VS. THE WORD OF GOD

When trying to discern a true or false prophet, it is important to remember that the timing issue was never addressed in the Word of God. He never said:

*"If a prophet speaks a word in my name, and it doesn't come to pass... wait awhile. I mean, you never know WHEN it could happen! Don't judge the person who prophesies! He/She may be speaking something way out in the future!"*

No! This topic was never discussed! Instead, the method of discernment shown in the Word is much more black and white, which begs the question:

Why did the timing issue never come up? Could it be that God never really wanted us to consider it in the first place?

This should give us something to think about.

God was very specific in His Word. He spoke of a "method of discernment" that was very absolute, and I believe that we should be just as strict with our judgments as well. It doesn't matter how much we identify with said prophet. It doesn't matter how nice he is or how sweet her words sound.

God gave us His Word to obey. He did not give us the Word so that we can apply our human reasoning to it and rationalize it away.

## A PRESUMPTUOUS PROPHET IS NOT WORTHY OF HONOR

The Bible says that if someone prophesies something that fails to come to pass, we are to have nothing to do with that person.

Let's take another look at **Deuteronomy 18:20-22**:

> *But the prophet who presumes to speak a word in My name, which I have not commanded him to speak, or who speaks in the name of other gods, that prophet shall die.*
>
> *And if you say in your heart, "How shall we know the word which the LORD has not spoken?"*
>
> *When a prophet speaks in the name of the LORD, if the thing does not happen or come to pass, that [is] the thing which the LORD has not spoken; the prophet has spoken it presumptuously; you shall not be afraid of him.*

In translating *"you shall not be afraid,"* the word **"guwr"** [H1481][4] was used. It means to "keep company with," "abide with," as well as "be afraid of" and "stand in awe of."

Whatever definition you pick, the prophet who has spoken falsely (the "false prophet") is a person who is not worthy of honor or adoration in any way. This may be very harsh to our western sensibilities, but it is truth, nonetheless.

While it should be obvious that we should treat people with kindness and civility, we need to also realize that there is a big difference between being nice to and honoring someone. Much like there is a big difference between being friendly and developing a companionship with a person.

If I came into contact with a false prophet, I would say "Hi," and be cordial just like I would with any other person. I might even smile. But I definitely wouldn't go over to his house for a barbeque or let him know I approve of his twisted ways.

I would not honor him because he is misrepresenting my King.

Likewise, you should not be afraid to call out those who walk and talk in presumption, especially if it is backed up by two or three witnesses from Scripture.

We are called to protect those who are falling into the trap of the enemy, not to endorse those who cause them to stumble.

**Footnotes:**

[1] Webster's Definition of the word "presume" -
http://dictionary.reference.com/browse/presume?s=t

[2] Blueletter Bible definition of the word "zadown" [H2087]
https://www.blueletterbible.org/lang/lexicon/lexicon.cfm?Strongs=H2087&t=KJV

[3] Blueletter Bible definition of the word "zuwd" [H2102]
https://www.blueletterbible.org/lang/lexicon/lexicon.cfm?strongs=H2102&t=KJV

[4] Blueletter Bible definition of the word "guwr" [H1481]
https://www.blueletterbible.org/lang/lexicon/lexicon.cfm?strongs=H1481&t=KJV

# SCRIPTURAL WITNESS #4: FALSE PROPHETS LEAD YOU AWAY FROM GOD'S COMMANDS

The next principle from scripture that I am going to discuss has the potential to eliminate most modern-day prophets from any list that is out there. This may be the one principle in this entire book that will get the most flack.

For this reason, I would like to lay some groundwork before I get into the "meat" of this chapter. Let us lay down some basic, immovable "pillars" in our doctrine.

Can we all agree that:

- *God doesn't change?* (**Malachi 3:6**)

- *Jesus Christ is the same yesterday, today and forever?* (**Hebrews 13:8**)

- *Jesus was the exact representation of the Father?* (**Hebrews 1:3**)

- *Jesus spoke the Father's Words?* (**John 14:10**)

As professed believers in Jesus as the Messiah, the pillars above should be "givens" for all of us. Let's see if we can add just a few more points of agreement.

- *Sin is disobedience to God's Law.* (**1 John 3:4**)

- *Jesus came to save us from our sin.* (**Matthew 1:21**)

- *Repentance is turning away from sin.* (**Acts 3:19**)

- *In the New Covenant, we have God's Law in our hearts and minds.* **(Jeremiah 31:33)**

If we can agree on these basic pillars, then this chapter will probably make sense to you. However, if you find yourself rationalizing these points with sentences that start with "Yeah, but...." then you may have a problem.

Still with me? Good! Let's move forward...

## PROPHECY IS NOT ABOUT PREDICTING THE FUTURE

People have been trained for years to focus on the prophet's ability to foretell future events or to know what is generally unknown about a person (aka "read people's mail"). This is NOT the reason the gift of prophecy has been given to us.

Throughout the Old and New Testament, all of the prophets had one central Message. If you will allow me to paraphrase, it went a little something like this:

*God is returning to set up His Kingdom! Repent from your wicked ways and return to His Ways! Obey His commands - all of them! If you do, GOOD things will happen! If you refuse, BAD things will happen!*

Every one of God's prophets (Moses, Elijah, Isaiah, Jeremiah, Ezekiel, John the Baptist, Jesus, et al) preached along these lines. Their unified message was a hardcore message of repentance to a disobedient people, pleading with them to turn from their wicked ways and obey the commands of God so that they could be blessed.

Of course, once the Messiah came, the prophets would also preach that He was the One who fulfilled many of the prophecies spoken of by the prophets of the past, but the core message of repentance was never eliminated. God was (and is) always calling people to repent of their sinful ways so that they could (and can) know and follow His Way.

Likewise, as God's "spokesman," the core of a prophet's message is repentance. The ability to foretell future events has always taken (and should always take) a backseat to this vital component of God's message to mankind.

## GOD GAVE US A "PLUMB LINE" FOR DISCERNING A PROPHET

The Father gave to the children of Israel (and us) ironclad instructions for discerning between true and false prophets.

### Deuteronomy 13:1-5

*If there arises among you a prophet or a dreamer of dreams, <u>and he gives you a sign or a wonder</u>, and the sign or the wonder comes to pass, of which he spoke to you, saying, 'Let us go after other gods' –which you have not known– 'and let us serve them,' <u>you shall not listen to the words of that prophet or that dreamer of dreams</u>, for <u>the LORD your God is testing you</u> to know whether you love the LORD your God with all your heart and with all your soul.*

*You shall walk after the LORD your God and fear Him, and <u>keep His commands and obey His voice</u>; you shall serve Him and hold fast to Him. But that prophet or that dreamer of dreams shall be put to death, <u>because he has spoken in order to turn [you] away from the LORD your God</u>, who brought you out of the land of Egypt and redeemed you from the house of bondage, <u>to entice you from the way in which the LORD your God commanded you to walk</u>. So you shall put away the evil from your midst.*

This passage is pretty straightforward. God is telling us that we are to ignore the prophet who entices us away from His commands ... **even if he/she performs signs and wonders**!

When signs and wonders are performed *apart from* a message of repentance from sin and turning back to God's Commands, they are no longer validations of a person's ministry **(Mark 16:17)**. They become tests from God!

*Do you love Him enough to walk in His commands, or not?*

So who would ever dare to try and entice us away from God's commands? Shouldn't we be able to spot these people easily?

Yes, we should, but unfortunately, this hasn't been happening.

## FALSE PROPHETS ENTICE US BY MANIPULATING THE WORDS OF GOD

Today's false prophets will never come right out and say, *"Hey! Let's go serve Baal instead of God!"* Instead, they subtly manipulate the Word of God to fit their particular prophecies, changing it to say what THEY want it to say. This hidden deception is disguised with soft, eloquent and CONVINCING speech that will affect a person emotionally, if they don't know the Word.

If weeping, exhilaration or excitement appears, a false prophet will quickly attribute it to the Spirit of God, and the sheep will believe the claim because they "felt" something.

God told us early on in Scripture:

> **Deuteronomy 4:2**
> *You shall not <u>add to</u> the word which I command you, nor <u>take from</u> it, that you may keep the commands of the LORD your God which I command you.*

This instruction can be used as a rock-solid foundation for us to stand on, when discerning false prophets and prophecy.

Everything that would be considered "the Word of God" from that time forth **MUST** line up and agree with God's original words to the children of Israel.

That means that NONE of the prophets' writings, Jesus' words in the Gospels, nor any of Paul's epistles can contradict God's words in the Old Testament - otherwise they would count as *adding to* and/or *diminishing* God's words.

A false prophet (and a false teacher) will cherry-pick a verse or two out of the New Testament, take it out of its context and create a whole doctrine out of it. And because the masses think "Well, hey... it's in the Bible," they will swallow the lie without the slightest hesitation.

Little do they know that they are being enticed to depart from the ways of our unchangeable God. The Bible attributes this to *"the spirit of harlotry."*

**Hosea 4:12b**
*For the spirit of harlotry has caused them to stray, and they have played the harlot against their God.*

What would a harlot do? She would offer you a false intimacy without a covenant. In church services where this alleged "prophetic spirit" is being manifested, there is indeed an "intimacy" that takes place, but it is deceptive in nature. You can definitely "feel" something flowing. It affects your emotions, your thoughts, and even your equilibrium. If you do not have a solid foundation in the Word of God, it is likely that you will be led to believe that what you are feeling is actually God's Holy Spirit, because it feels so good to your flesh.

But a false intimacy is not the only manifestation of the spirit of harlotry in the prophetic movement. Other manifestations such as sexual promiscuity, homosexuality, addiction, compromise and other lewd behaviors occur frequently behind closed doors.

Because the false prophets will not preach repentance or the true Word of God, this spirit of harlotry is allowed to enter in and wreak havoc in churches, leading multitudes astray.

## FALSE PROPHETS ENTICE US BY GETTING OUR FOCUS OFF OF GOD'S WORD

The false prophets preach a message that focuses on anything BUT the commands of God. The message of repentance is cheapened (or outright ignored). The commands of the Most High are considered obsolete, or "done away with."

Turning your attention from the written Word of God, the false prophet will get you to pursue other loves, other phenomena (feathers, gems, glory clouds) and other extra-biblical spiritual exercises... all under the pretense of having a new revelation, prophecy, or a special anointing from God.

Just like the Pharisees of old, false prophets will subtly promote and amplify their man-made doctrines (in the form of new revelation, etc.) OVER the Word of God.

This also causes congregations to open wide the door for the spirit of harlotry to enter.

### Hosea 5:4
*They do not direct their deeds toward turning to their God, for the spirit of harlotry is in their midst, and they do not know the LORD.*

**....They DO NOT know the Lord...**

Ouch! What an indictment against our modern day prophetic churches! These verses in Hosea mirror the words that Jesus will speak to the false prophets on that day.

**Matthew 7:23**
*And then I will declare to them, "I never knew you; depart from Me, you who practice lawlessness!"*

## WALKING AWAY FROM THE COMMANDS IS HARLOTRY

Like Satan tempting the Son of God in the wilderness, false prophets will only remain true to the Word of God if it builds their own kingdoms. If speaking the Word of God is going to penalize their finances or popularity, they will find ways to twist the Word so that the masses will be satisfied and their "ministries" remain intact. They may say things that SOUND like His Words; they may even SOUND loving and filled with supernatural lingo - but their purpose is to distract you and lead you AWAY from His commands and lead you TOWARD the "newer revelation" or "divine insight" of the speaker.

If you read the Word of God, you will find that He always equates walking away from His commands with spiritual harlotry (or adultery). There is no gray area - it's black and white. And if YOUR God doesn't change and MY God doesn't change, He still sees it the same way!

When a prophet boasts of divine revelation or a message from heaven, it should get your attention. If the message leads you to repentance and a desire to reverence and obey God's commands, that's a good message.

If, however, it leads you in any other direction, the "red lights" should be going off in your spirit.

You see, the prophet may or may not realize it, but when his "divine revelation" does not call the people back to God's commands, he is implying that his own "revelation" is more important than obedience to what God wrote long ago through the hand of His servant Moses (and the prophets who came after him).

The prophet's message may sound appealing and feel good, but in the end, it's all harlotry.

Take the words of this true prophet to heart, for they are still applicable today.

**Hosea 4:6**
*My people are destroyed for lack of knowledge. Because you have rejected knowledge, I also will reject you from being priest for Me; <u>Because you have forgotten the law of your God, I also will forget your children</u>.*

# SCRIPTURAL WITNESS #5: FALSE PROPHETS MIMIC THE SPIRIT OF GOD

The inescapable truth is that false prophets need to feel validated.

False prophets and their followers love to put on outward shows so others will think that the Holy Spirit is moving upon them. Often, this is demonstrated by various jerks, quakes, nonsensical phrases[1] and other odd spiritual manifestations.

Search for the term "drunk in the spirit" or "holy laughter" on YouTube and watch some of the videos that come up in the search results. If you do this, you'll see how this strange phenomenon works, between false prophets, their fans and whatever spirits they are entertaining.

It will probably also confuse you, and cause you to ask:

## "IS THIS THE HOLY SPIRIT, OR IS IT SOMETHING ELSE?"

Is it even possible to operate under the influence of the Holy Spirit? The answer is a resounding YES!

In this chapter, I want to show you from Scripture how to discern whether an alleged prophet is operating under the influence of the Holy Spirit or another spirit. I also want to give you some solid scriptural guidelines to help you determine if a spiritual manifestation is a fake - a deception, or the real deal.

But before I do that, I want to give you a little insight into a false prophet's rationale for acting the way they do. Their reasoning is as twisted as the spirits they serve.

## MANIFESTATIONS AND THE OLD TESTAMENT PROPHET

When deceiving others, it is always in a false prophet's best interest to quickly silence any questions or opposition from those who may suspect that these manifestations are something other than the Holy Spirit.

One way they do this is by claiming that the Holy Spirit manifested physical, outward signs through the Old Testament prophets. For example, Isaiah walked around naked and Ezekiel laid siege to the model of Jerusalem while lying on his side. Those signs were definitely odd.

Hey, if the Old Testament prophets could act oddly, why can't they?

This reasoning exhibits a high level of hypocrisy and inconsistency because these same people who aspire to be just like Old Testament prophets (by manifesting things outwardly) quickly rationalize, or outright REJECT, the Old Testament prophet's message, which was inspired by the SAME Holy Spirit as those in the New Testament.

Embracing the odd behavior of the Old Testament prophets because it supports their idea of what "manifesting the Holy Spirit" looks like, they consider the MESSAGE of those same men of God to be "Old Covenant" stuff, and not worthy of consideration.

Adopting select Old Testament prophetic Scriptures but rejecting the prophetic message (not to mention ignoring the entire context) of those Scriptures is a favored tactic of the modern day false prophet. They LOVE to adopt certain Scriptures and concepts that will suit a particular purpose, but they will marginalize or outright REJECT others.

As you study the superior message of the true prophets in the Word of God, you will notice a vast difference between their message and the message of false prophets.

The message of a real prophet will ALWAYS lead you to repentance and draw you back to obedience to His written Word. A false prophet's message will ALWAYS lead you someplace else.

Indeed, they are the "pied pipers" of our time.

### Isaiah 8:20
*To the law and to the testimony! If they do not speak according to this word, it is because there is no light in them.*

I really like how the New Living Translation renders this verse.

### Isaiah 8:20
*Look to God's instructions and teachings! People who contradict his word are completely in the dark.*

## BUT I'M JUST A HELPLESS MARIONETTE!

Unlike the false prophets of today, the physical manifestations of the Old Testament prophets were performed while they were in complete control of their faculties.

As they conveniently sidestep **1 Corinthians 14:33**, which states *"God is not the author of confusion, but of peace,"* the false prophets will claim that the Holy Spirit is ordering and controlling them, in essence "forcing" them to manifest this bizarre behavior.

Do you really think that God forced Isaiah to walk around naked? **(Isaiah 20:2)** No, He didn't. Isaiah had a choice.

Ezekiel even changed God's mind as to how a manifestation was going to be performed! God originally wanted Ezekiel to cook his food over human dung! But Ezekiel couldn't handle it (who could?) so God had him cook it over cow dung (um, gee… thanks God). **(Ezekiel 4:12-15)**

Let's read **1 Corinthians 14:33** in its fullness.

> **1 Corinthians 14:33**
> … *and the spirits of the prophets are subject* **[G5293 – hypotasso]** *to the prophets. For God is not the author of confusion, but of peace, as in all churches of the saints.*

The Greek word for "subject" is **hypotasso [G5293]**[2], which means subordinate, put in subjection, and obedient.

Before I continue, I have to ask the following questions:

- *Did you feel peace as you watched the spiritual drunkenness videos?*

- *Did the people have their spirits subordinate or in subjection?*

   *…or….*

- *Was it chaotic and maybe just a bit self-serving?*

Think about it…. Selah!

So, if a spiritual manifestation does not come from the Holy Spirit, where does it come from?

Well, there are a few possibilities.

## MANIFESTATIONS THAT ARE FLESHLY IN NATURE

Because of their insatiable need for affirmation, a false prophet may invent this stuff, purely for the sake of keeping the audience intrigued.

False prophets have also been known take advantage of a well-known dynamic that takes place in prophetic conferences, prayer groups, etc. Here's what happens.

If a prophet appears to be "manifesting the Holy Spirit," his followers will voluntarily (or sometimes involuntarily) mimic their behavior, kicking it into high gear once they notice people are watching. The false prophet who wants to start a scene knows that this will happen.

During this time, it is difficult to know who is faking it and who is under the influence of a spirit, but one thing is certain, *nobody* is repenting or returning to God with a humble and contrite heart.

This happens more often than most people want to admit, and it's all centered around self-promotion (of both the speaker and the follower).

**1 Corinthians 14:33** states that *"God is not the author of confusion."* I believe **James 3:16** adds some insight.

> **James 3:16**
> *For where envying and strife* **[G2052 – eritheia]** *is, there is confusion and every evil work.*

Although the word eritheia can mean "strife," its primary definition has to do more with "putting one's self forward" or "self promotion," than it does "causing division."[3]

Self-promotion (along with strife) and confusion always walk hand-in-hand - along with *"every evil work."*

This ties in closely with Scriptural Witness #2. A false prophet will do *anything* to keep the crowd following them, including faking it when they see an advantage in doing so.

But not all manifestations are fleshly!

## SOME MANIFESTATIONS OCCUR THAT ARE ENTIRELY SPIRITUAL IN NATURE.

Because they have opened the door for the spirit of harlotry to enter their services (see Scriptural Witness #4), prophetic churches are open to the manifestation of other spirits as well. Many of the people who have given themselves over to these deceptive spirits end up possessed by what they *thought* was from God, but was actually a satanic counterfeit.

Spiritual manifestations such as these occurred during Paul's ministry. A girl possessed by the spirit of divination **[G4436 – python]**[4] followed Paul and company around saying really positive and encouraging things about them!

> **Acts 16:16-18**
> *Now it happened, as we went to prayer, that a certain slave girl possessed with a spirit of divination* **[G4436 – python]** *met us, who brought her masters much profit by fortune-telling* **[G3132 – manteuomai]**.
>
> *This girl followed Paul and us, and cried out, saying, "These men are the servants of the Most High God, who proclaim to us the way of salvation."*
>
> *And this she did for many days. But Paul, greatly annoyed, turned and said to the spirit, "I command you*

*in the name of Jesus Christ to come out of her." And he came out that very hour.*

The Greek word translated as "fortune-telling" is **manteuomai [G3132]**[5] actually means *"to prophesy like a seer"!* (See footnotes.)

Let's take this just a little deeper.

The root word for **manteuomai** is **mainomai [G3105]**[6] which means "to rant and rave" like you are out of your mind!

So let's work these definitions into the story.

This girl was possessed by the spirit of python [divination]. Prophesying like a seer, she made a lot of money for her masters. Apparently, she was really good at her job of mimicking the prophetic gift.

Seeing the successful ministry of the apostles, she was quick to recognize an opportunity to be noticed. Jumping on their coattails, she followed them, crying out "These men are the servants of the Most High God, who proclaim to us the way of salvation."

"Ranting and raving" like a lunatic, she proclaimed TRUE things about Paul and his disciples.

It was true that they were servants of the Most High, and it was true that they proclaimed the Way of Salvation to the people. Notice that the girl was able to say all these things - even while under the influence of a spirit other than the Holy Spirit.

But this really annoyed Paul. Why?

Because she was operating under a false prophetic gifting. She was "prophesying" **(manteuomai [G3132])** under the influence of a spirit of divination (python). It appeared as if she were supporting God's Work, but in truth she was destroying it by bringing attention to man and not calling people to repentance! If she were truly prophesying by the Spirit of God, she would have been calling people back to God's commands, not bringing attention to something or someone else.

We have the same type of false prophets behind (and in front of) pulpits today, who speak accurate words and loudly sing the praises of God, yet they operate under a strong spirit of divination (python). You can recognize them by their words (again, see Scriptural Witness #4) as well as their manifestations.

## MANIFESTATIONS THAT ARE BOTH PHYSICAL AND SPIRITUAL IN NATURE

Prophetic manifestations can also be a combination of both physical AND spiritual forces. This is a particularly harmful situation, because it means that a demonic spirit and the flesh are working together. The demonic spirit no longer needs to exert control over this person because he/she is freely, willfully and independently submitting to the will of that spirit.

We see a perfect example of this in the false prophet Zedekiah. (Read all of **1 Kings 22** for context).

> **1 Kings 22:11**
> *Now Zedekiah the son of Chenaanah had made horns of iron <u>for himself</u>; and he said, "Thus says the LORD: 'With these you shall gore the Syrians until they are destroyed.'"*

This part of the passage shows a physical manifestation performed by Zedekiah. The false prophet was not forced by any spirit to make the horns of iron; he just wanted to put on an elaborate show for the kings. He wanted to show the kings and the people in the court, "Hey, the spirit is on me!"

To the dismay of King Ahab (and Zedekiah), the true prophet Micaiah countered this prophecy and gave a negative report based upon what the Spirit of God showed him.

> **1 Kings 22:17**
> *And he said, "I saw all Israel scattered upon the hills, as sheep that have not a shepherd: and the LORD said, 'These have no master: let them return every man to his house in peace.'"*

Nowadays, if Micaiah had given a real prophetic word in one of our prophetic churches, he would have been either ignored or dismissed as an angry prophet in need of a revelation of God's grace.

As part of Micaiah's negative report, God gave Zedekiah, Jehoshaphat, Ahab and us a glimpse behind the scenes of what was occurring in the spirit realm, as well as a deeper understanding of how false prophets cooperate with a lying spirit.

> **1 Kings 22:19-23**
> *And he said, "Hear thou therefore the word of the LORD: I saw the LORD sitting on his throne, and all the host of heaven standing by him on his right hand and on his left.*
>
> *And the LORD said, 'Who shall persuade Ahab, that he may go up and fall at Ramoth Gilead?' And one said on this manner, and another said on that manner.*
>
> *And there came forth a spirit, and stood before the LORD, and said, 'I will persuade him.'*

*And the LORD said unto him, 'Wherewith?' And he said, 'I will go forth, and I will be a lying spirit in the mouth of all his prophets.' And he said, 'Thou shalt persuade him, and prevail also: go forth, and do so.'*

*Now therefore, behold, the LORD hath put a lying spirit in the mouth of all these thy prophets, and the LORD hath spoken evil concerning thee."*

Notice that it is God who puts the lying spirit in the mouth of the false prophets? I wish I could go down this rabbit trail, but this passage in **1 Kings 22:23** ties directly in to **Deuteronomy 13:1-5** and **2 Thessalonians 2** (particularly **verses 11-12**). I'll leave you to study it out on your own.

So we see that Zedekiah made horns of iron using his own free will, but then God sent a lying spirit and spoke through his lips. It's the perfect combination.

Was Zedekiah deceived?

Obviously... but I believe that Zedekiah "thought" he was doing the right thing. I don't think he was intentionally trying to be malicious and deceive the king.

Hmmmm.... that sounds familiar. **(See Scriptural Witness #1.)**

## THE MANIFESTATION "HOT BUTTON"

No matter if it is spiritual, physical or both, the issue of "manifesting the Holy Spirit" is a real sensitive topic for many wrapped up in the prophetic movement. They have been trained to believe that *any* spiritual activity that gives them a good feeling *must* be from God, so there is a lot of misguided zeal (to put it gently). If you question the validity of these manifestations, things can get ugly really quickly, or even violent.

<u>Nobody wants to be confronted with (or admit to) the fact that they may be manifesting a lying demon, or just plain lying.</u>

This same type of situation occurred in **1 Kings**. The false prophet Zedekiah, although he may have meant well, did NOT like to hear that he was under the influence of a lying spirit!

### 1 Kings 22:24
*Now Zedekiah the son of Chenaanah went near and struck Micaiah on the cheek, and said, "Which way did the spirit from the LORD go from me to speak to you?"*

## I WANT TO TALK A LITTLE MORE ABOUT "SPIRITUAL DRUNKENNESS"

One of the main spiritual manifestations of our day is what is known as "spiritual drunkenness."

Although there may be a few fakers in the bunch (especially among the prophets who like to create this atmosphere), I believe that this manifestation is primarily spiritual in nature. People who participate in what have come to be known as "Holy Ghost Parties" sincerely believe they are feeling, partaking of, or interacting with the Holy Spirit. What they don't realize is that they are actually reaping God's punishment.

### Isaiah 29:9-10
*Pause and wonder!*
*Blind yourselves and be blind!*
*They are drunk, but not with wine;*
*They stagger, but not with intoxicating drink.*
*For the LORD has poured out on you*
*The spirit of deep sleep,*

*And has closed your eyes, namely, the prophets;*
*And He has covered your heads, namely, the seers.*

Do a study. Search for the words "drunk" and "drunkenness" in the writings of the prophets. It's almost always associated with God's wrath and deception.

Of course, the false prophets have their scriptures too. Sometimes they will bring up the following verse in order to justify their behavior.

### Ephesians 5:18
*And do not be drunk with wine, in which is dissipation; but be filled with the Spirit…*

They translate this verse to mean that being filled with the Spirit is an alternative to being drunk (or high) and that, somehow, it will have the same effect. But (as usual) they do not consider the rest of the scripture.

### Ephesians 5:18-21
*And do not be drunk with wine, in which is dissipation [**asotia – G810**]; but be filled with the Spirit, speaking to one another in psalms and hymns and spiritual songs, singing and making melody in your heart to the Lord, giving thanks always for all things to God the Father in the name of our Lord Jesus Christ, submitting to one another in the fear of God.*

A life that is characterized by being filled with the Spirit is a life full of speaking and singing to each other and God, being thankful and submitting to one another *"in the fear of God."*

## WHAT DOES IT MEAN TO SUBMIT TO ONE ANOTHER "IN THE FEAR OF GOD?"

How do you submit to each other "in the fear of God?" This does not mean that you submit to each other BECAUSE you fear God's punishment if you don't.

The Bible states:

> **Proverbs 8:13**
> *The fear of the LORD IS to hate evil; pride and arrogance and the evil way and the perverse mouth I hate.*

So, we submit to one another "in the fear of God" with hating evil as a *primary* objective.

It is right for me to submit to my brother and sister if they tell me that I am breaking the commandments of God, and they should submit to me as well. Together, we *hate* evil and do everything possible to be rid of it in our lives.

That is how you submit to each other *"in the fear of God."*

The Word of God states:

> **1 Peter 1:13-14**
> *Therefore gird up the loins of your mind, be SOBER, and rest your hope fully upon the grace that is to be brought to you at the revelation of Jesus Christ; as obedient children, not conforming yourselves to the former lusts, as in your ignorance;*

## "NOT CONFORMING YOURSELVES TO THE FORMER LUSTS."

A lot of these people that manifest this type of drunken behavior are children of the 60's and/or former druggies of a more recent vintage.

There's a connection here.

If the enemy cannot entice you to open your mind (or spirit) up through actual drug use, he will entice you to open your mind (or spirit) up through a spiritual imitation. Both methods accomplish the same purpose by causing you to drop your guard so that the enemy can come in and do his bidding.

> **2 Timothy 2:25-26**
> *In meekness instructing those that oppose themselves; if God peradventure will give them repentance to the acknowledging of the truth; and that they may recover themselves out of the snare of the devil, who are taken captive by him at his will.*

Demonic spirits are MORE than able to affect a person's thoughts and emotions (even physical being) if his/her mind is not renewed according to the written Word of God, or if they are consistently walking in some form of disobedience.

## WHEN GOD REALLY TOUCHES YOU

After reading all of this, don't get the idea that that God can't (or won't) move upon an individual, even to the point of a physical manifestation. Believe me, if the King of the Universe comes into contact with dirt (you and me), something is gonna move. At the same time, something is going to be changed forever!

So, in summary, if you see a bunch of "moving and shaking" going on with an alleged prophet (or his followers) with no lasting change in their lives… if you hear "word" after "word" after endless "word" without any righteous effect in the hearers, you can pretty much count on it being a bunch of hooey.

There may be signs, wonders and lots of "God-talk," but if they are not leading you to "God's instructions and teachings," it is because they are *completely in the dark."* **(Isaiah 8:20 NLT)**

Selah.

**Footnotes**

[1]  I'm not referring to speaking in tongues.

[2]  Blueletter Bible definition of the word "hypotasso" [G5239]
https://www.blueletterbible.org/lang/lexicon/lexicon.cfm?Strongs=G5293&t=KJV

[3]  Blueletter Bible definition of the word "eritheia" [G2052]
https://www.blueletterbible.org/lang/lexicon/lexicon.cfm?Strongs=G2052&t=KJV

[4]  Blueletter Bible definition of the word "python" [G4436]
https://www.blueletterbible.org/lang/lexicon/lexicon.cfm?Strongs=G4436&t=KJV

[5]  Blueletter Bible definition of the word "manteuomai" [G3132]
https://www.blueletterbible.org/lang/lexicon/lexicon.cfm?Strongs=G3132&t=KJV

[6] Blueletter Bible definition of the word "mainomai" [G3105]
https://www.blueletterbible.org/lang/lexicon/lexicon.cfm?Strongs=G3105&t=KJV

# SCRIPTURAL WITNESS #6: FALSE PROPHETS HAVE FALSE DREAMS AND VISIONS (PART 1)

Have you ever sat and listened silently to a prophet or prophetess expound upon what seemed to be the latest of an endless series of dreams or visions? Were you tempted to question the veracity of their encounter(s), only to be silenced by echoes of *"touch not God's anointed"* coursing through your mind?

Believe me, I have.

Let me tell you what God's Word has to say about false prophets and their dreams and visions.

## PEOPLE ARE DESPERATE FOR SOMETHING BEYOND THEIR REALITY

Dreams and visions are a legitimate part of the prophetic experience; however, false prophets also use these same phenomena as tools to keep their audiences mesmerized. They know that nothing captures the attention and allegiance of desperate seekers more than stories about dreams and visions of angels, heavenly encounters and open gates.

We are all hungry for something beyond our perception of reality and, because of this hunger, those who claim to have "been there" will always find an audience among those who have not made the Word their foundation.

How can we know if what they are saying is the "Real Deal" or just a fabrication? Did these prophets really have a legitimate prophetic encounter with God in a dream or vision, or was it a clever delusion?

We all dream and, from time to time, drift off into our imaginations and daydreams. I don't know about you, but sometimes my experiences can be surprisingly vivid.

How can we tell if the dreams and visions that WE experience are from God, or are just the result of too much pizza from the night before?

I will be providing some scriptural guidelines in this chapter and the next.

## DREAMS, VISIONS AND THE PROPHET

Dreams and visions are valid ways in which God communicates with His prophets. In the book of Numbers, the Most High said that He would make Himself known to a prophet in a dream, or speak to him in a vision.

> **Numbers 12:6**
> *Then He said, "Hear now My words: If there is a prophet among you, I, the LORD, make Myself known to him in a vision; I speak to him in a dream."*

Read this verse again and notice where it says *"If there is a prophet among you?"*

There are conditions that need to be met, in order for God to consider you a prophet. For starters, God says that He needs to contact you through either a dream or a vision.

Now, this verse does not say that EVERYONE God contacts through dreams or visions is a prophet.

Abimelech **(Genesis 20:3)**, Laban the Syrian **(Genesis 31:24)**, Pharaoh **(Genesis 41:25)**, the pagan king Nebuchadnezzar **(Daniel 4)** and Joseph **(Matthew 2:12)** are all examples of people God contacted through dreams and visions who were NOT prophets.

There is something special about the **WAY** God reveals Himself to a prophet that sets his experience apart from the rest and enables him to prophesy.

## WHEN THE MOST HIGH PUTS HIS WORDS IN YOUR MOUTH

### Jeremiah 1:9-10
*Then the LORD put forth His hand and touched my mouth, and the LORD said to me: "<u>Behold, I have put My words in your mouth</u>. See, I have this day set you over the nations and over the kingdoms, to root out and to pull down, to destroy and to throw down, to build and to plant."*

According to God's Word, if He has contacted you through a dream or a vision, and He has put His Words in your mouth, then it validates your standing as a prophet.

God encourages true prophets to faithfully speak the Words that He communicates to them (either in a dream, or otherwise) as His representative.

### Jeremiah 23:28
*The prophet that hath a dream, let him tell a dream; and he that hath my word, let him speak my word faithfully.*

But there is a "flip side" to this situation.

Just like God encourages His prophets to speak His Words (either by dreams or otherwise), He is against those who tell false dreams and visions. His Word is very clear about this.

### Jeremiah 23:32
*"Behold, <u>I am against those who prophesy false dreams</u>," says the LORD, "and tell them, and <u>cause My people to err by their lies and by their recklessness</u>. Yet I did not send them or command them; therefore they shall not profit this people at all," says the LORD.*

### Jeremiah 23:25-26
*I have heard what the prophets have said who prophesy lies in My name, saying, "I have dreamed, I have dreamed!" How long shall this be in the heart of the prophets that prophesy lies? Yea, they are prophets of the deceit of their own heart;*

Why is God against people telling false dreams? Because they cause His people to fall into error... more on this later.

## DISCERNING BETWEEN THE TRUE AND FALSE

Since we don't want to walk in error, it is of the utmost importance that we learn to discern between true and false dreams and visions. So how can we discern whether or not the prophet's dreams and visions are inspired by the Holy Spirit or just their own delusion? "Who" or "what" has the right to determine whether a dream is inspired or carnal?

Hopefully by now, we've all arrived at the conclusion that the Word of God is the answer and that we, through renewed minds, can make that determination.

### Romans 12:2
*And be not conformed to this world: but be ye*

*transformed by the renewing of your mind, that **ye may prove** what is that good, and acceptable, and perfect, will of God.*

I'm going to be straight with you. The truth is, I haven't found much detail in the Word of God on what constitutes a true dream or vision. I'm not saying that it isn't to be found, I'm just saying that, so far, it hasn't been revealed to me yet. However, there are *many* details regarding false dreams and visions.

So, if we research and look to see what God has to say about *false* dreams and visions, I believe that we can learn about the specifics of *true* dreams and visions by identifying the *opposite* specifics of the false. Does that make sense?

## FALSE DREAMS AND VISIONS
## WILL NOT EXPOSE SIN

In Lamentations, the prophet Jeremiah "laments" the demise of Jerusalem. Because they refused to obey God's Law and went after the idols of the surrounding nations, the Chosen People were taken captive by the Babylonians. With the exception of a few, they were *"vomited"* out of the Promised Land.

What was a major contributor to this geographical nausea?

### Lamentations 2:14
*Your prophets have seen for you false and deceptive visions; they have not uncovered your iniquity, to bring back your captives, but have envisioned for you false prophecies and delusions.*

From this verse, we can see that a false and deceptive vision lacks the substance that will expose iniquity. So we need to ask ourselves – do the dreams and visions of our modern day prophets expose our sin? If they do not, then we are being deceived - and cheated, I might add.

According to Lamentations, when iniquity is uncovered, the captives return to their land.

The modern day church, spiritually, has been in captivity to our sins for way too long, grossly ignoring God's commands and pursuing other gods. Over the centuries, we've been conditioned to listen to self-appointed leaders who refuse to hate what God hates, and our flesh has gladly played along.

Because our iniquity has not been uncovered, we remain in spiritual captivity. We bring reproach to the Father in the sight of the pagans, demonstrating clearly that we are no different than they are. One day, if we continue to listen to false dreams and visions that ignore our need to repent, our spiritual captivity will result in actual physical captivity. Mark my words.

## FALSE DREAMS AND VISIONS
## GIVE YOU FALSE PEACE

In a time when the Judgment of God is imminent, false dreams and visions will assure you that nothing bad is going to happen, because (like Israel), *"You are God's chosen – you have no need to fear and there is no consequence for your sin."*

> ### Jeremiah 23:16-17
> *Thus says the LORD of hosts: "Do not listen to the words of the prophets who prophesy to you. They make you worthless; they speak a vision of their own heart, not from the mouth of the LORD. They continually say to those who despise Me, 'The LORD has said, "You shall have peace;"' and to everyone who walks according to the dictates of his own heart, they say, 'No evil shall come upon you.'"* **(Also see Jeremiah 8:8-11.)**

When false prophets tell of dreams and visions, they may say that they are aiming to heal and unify the people, but in truth, these are only verbal claims geared toward appeasing the fear of man and increasing their fan bases.

The false prophets of the Old Testament were guilty of the same crime.

> **Jeremiah 6:13-15**
> *Because from the least of them even to the greatest of them, everyone is given to covetousness; and <u>from the prophet even to the priest, everyone deals falsely</u> [sheqer – H8267].*[1]
>
> *They have also healed [rapha – H7495][2] the hurt [sheber – H7667][3] of My people slightly [qalal – H7043][4], saying, 'Peace, peace!' when there is no peace.*
>
> *Were they ashamed when they had committed abomination? No! They were not at all ashamed; nor did they know how to blush. Therefore they shall fall among those who fall; at the time I punish them, they shall be cast down," says the LORD.*

I have provided links to the original Hebrew words in the footnotes of this chapter for your own study. What this scripture is actually saying is that the prophets and priests were putting a superficial salve on the "hurt" of the people. This "hurt" was not an injury to their persons (or their hearts), but it was their sin that caused a broken/shattered [sheber – H7667] covenant with their God. They were treating it as an insignificant issue, [qalal – H7043] so their sin went unexposed, and they did not repent. Therefore both the deceiver and the deceived would pay the consequence.

That is just like the false prophets of today. They treat our sin as a light issue, something easily overcome by the "grace of

God" without any action (repentance) or sacrifice (crucifying the flesh) on our part. In fact, today's false prophets are the *personification* of the Old Testament false prophets, who shouted *"Peace! Peace!"* to the disobedient when there would be no peace for them.

Why do they do this? Because just like the Old Testament false prophets, they are people-pleasers and man-fearers. They are far too concerned with their incomes and fan bases to actually deliver a true message from God. And the masses who think they believe in the Messiah do not want to hear a message of rebuke - ever.

## FALSE DREAMS AND VISIONS ARE WORTHLESS AND MAKE YOU WORTHLESS

When discerning whether or not a dream (or vision) is from God, it is important to look at what the dream (or vision) produces.

- *Does it motivate us to hunger for and pursue righteousness?*

- *Does it cause us to rid ourselves of sin so that we will be useful for His purposes?*

- *Does it further the Kingdom?*

....Or does it cause us to pursue the next supernatural experience?

Let's take another look at **Jeremiah 23**.

### Jeremiah 23:16-17
*Thus says the LORD of Hosts: "Do not listen to the words of the prophets who prophesy to you. They make you worthless; they speak a vision of their own heart, not from the mouth of the LORD. They continually say*

> *to those who despise Me, 'The LORD has said, "You shall have peace"'; and to everyone who walks according to the dictates of his own heart, they say, 'No evil shall come upon you.'"*

Throughout God's Word, we see that God measures your love for Him by how much you obey His commands. (For starters, see **1 John 5:2-3, John 14:15, 21.**) It is only logical that those who "despise" God and "follow the dictates of their own heart" are those who do NOT obey His commands. Yet these are the same people that the false prophets will assure, *"Hey! Don't worry about a thing! God loves you so much and He approves of you! You are a mighty warrior and will overcome the enemy.... and prosper... and signs and wonders will follow you wherever you go!!"*

Although they probably believe that they are building people up by speaking positive things over them, they are actually just inflating their egos and comforting them in their sin, which makes them worthless to the Master.

Don't get me wrong - there is definitely a time and place for encouragement, but in the realm of prophecy, encouragement only occurs when repentance, faithfulness and obedience are present. Otherwise, there should be strong rebuke.

Why the strong rebuke? Because God hates sin, and He won't use you if your life is not yielded to Him. But false prophets do not consider this. They would much rather "speak a vision of their own heart."

If false prophets *"walk according to the dictates of their own hearts,"* they will *"speak a vision"* that comes from the exact same place. And it is inevitable that a person's carnal dreams and visions are going to reflect their personal bents and the views of the people that they listen to.

Unfortunately, these views will only make those who listen to them **worthless** to the Kingdom of God. With no sense of urgency and a misguided image of God as exclusively "a God of Love," they will remain complacent, comfortable and unrepentant.

## FALSE DREAMS AND VISIONS CAUSE YOU TO FORGET GOD

The modern day church has promoted an image of God that does not line up with His Word at all. Along with self-appointed pastors who long to tell their congregations what they want to hear, the false prophets have complimented this image through their false dreams and visions.

Once again, we find that our modern day prophets look awfully similar to the Old Testament false prophets.

### Jeremiah 23:26-27
*How long will this be in the heart of the prophets who prophesy lies? Indeed they are prophets of the deceit of their own heart, <u>who try to make My people forget My name by their dreams which everyone tells his neighbor, as their fathers forgot My name for Baal</u>.*

There are a couple of points I want to make here.

In our Western way of thinking, we think of a person's name as merely a label. My name is Kevin, someone else is named Fred, and then, of course, there is Mary. In our minds, a name says nothing about a person's personality, reputation or deeds. It's all relative.

When the Bible refers to a person's name, it usually refers to the description of the entire person – especially when the Name of God is mentioned. It was not just a label. It was both a label and a reference to His entire character.

When Jeremiah was saying that a person's dream was causing people to forget God's Name, he was saying that these dreams were causing people to forget who God really was - His worth, His personality, His image, His mighty deeds, His likes and dislikes. False dreams were causing people to forget everything about Him!

Instead, they were forgetting God's "Name" and were replacing it with Baal's "name."

## WHO WAS BAAL?

Most of us have been told that Baal was the name of a god (or idol). This is not exactly a complete definition. If you worshipped Baal, it was not the same thing as worshipping Ashtoreth, Molech or the other named "gods" of the Old Testament.

Instead of being an individual "god" with a prescribed method of worship and a specific personality (for lack of a better term), "Baal" was a generalized name for any regional authority (spiritual or physical). Much like we use the term "God" to refer to the Being we serve (capitalizing it out of reverence) but the same term "god" can be used to describe any being of worship.

Here's what the Wikipedia entry says:

> Baal, also rendered Ba'al (Biblical Hebrew בַּעַל, pronounced ['baʕal]), is a North-West Semitic title and honorific meaning "master" or "lord" that is used for various gods who were patrons of cities in the Levant and Asia Minor, cognate to Akkadian Bēlu. A Baalist or Baalite means a worshipper of Baal.
>
> "Baal" may refer to any god and even to human officials. In some texts it is used for Hadad, a god of the

*rain, thunder, fertility and agriculture, and the lord of Heaven. Since only priests were allowed to utter his divine name, Hadad, Ba'al was commonly used. Nevertheless, few if any biblical uses of "Baal" refer to Hadad, the lord over the assembly of gods on the holy mount of Heaven; most refer to a variety of local spirit-deities worshiped as cult images, each called baal and regarded in the Hebrew Bible in that context as a "false god".* [5]

I'm saying all this to point out that false dreams have a way of making you forget who your God really is. Instead, they are heavily influenced by the "group think," image, or spiritual authority that resides over your area.

I don't claim to be extremely knowledgeable in the area of spiritual warfare (another used and abused topic of debate), but from what I have observed, the masses (within and outside the Western church) are held under the sway of politically correct thinking, which comes from some kind of deceiving spirit.

Anything that violates the image of tolerance is deemed to be offensive and wrong.

And it's in the church too. God is painted as someone who wants to go around and hug people all the time and wants us to do the same. This non-offensive, come as you are image of "god" is reinforced through the false dreams and visions of the prophets.

Instead of agreeing with the written Word of the Most High, false dreams and visions cause you to forget who He really is.

His Word says:

### Jeremiah 23:28-29

*"The prophet who has a dream, let him tell a dream; and he who has My word, let him speak My word faithfully. What is the chaff to the wheat?" says the LORD.*

*"Is not My word like <u>a fire</u>?" says the LORD, "And like <u>a hammer that breaks the rock in pieces</u>?"*

If you dare to deliver a Word that is like "fire" or "like a hammer that breaks the rock in pieces," be prepared for resistance. The modern day church will not view you as "full of grace and mercy."

**Footnotes:**

[1] Blueletter Bible definition of the word "sheqer" [H8267]
https://www.blueletterbible.org/lang/lexicon/lexicon.cfm?Strongs=H8267&t=KJV

[2] Blueletter Bible definition of the word "rapha" [H7495]
https://www.blueletterbible.org/lang/lexicon/lexicon.cfm?Strongs=H7495&t=KJV

[3] Blueletter Bible definition of the word "sheber" [H7667]
https://www.blueletterbible.org/lang/lexicon/lexicon.cfm?strongs=H7667&t=KJV

[4] Blueletter Bible definition of the word "qalal" [H7043]
https://www.blueletterbible.org/lang/lexicon/lexicon.cfm?strongs=H7043&t=KJV

[5] Wikipedia: https://en.wikipedia.org/wiki/Baal

# SCRIPTURAL WITNESS #6: FALSE PROPHETS HAVE FALSE DREAMS AND VISIONS (PART 2)

## HOW WILL I KNOW IF MY DREAMS AND VISIONS ARE FROM GOD?

As I said in the last chapter, there doesn't appear to be much information regarding legitimate dreams and visions from God in the Bible, but the opposite seems to be true of false (carnal) dreams and visions. So, if we study the Word and find aspects of the false, then we should logically derive the true characteristics by considering the opposite of what we find.

Let's review what we have learned and apply this technique.

What do we know about false dreams and visions?

- *False dreams and visions do not expose sin.*

- *False dreams and visions give you a false peace.*

- *False dreams and visions are worthless and make YOU worthless.*

- *False dreams and visions cause you to forget God.*

So, if the attributes of the false are accurate and they are, because it is verified by the Word, then we can derive the following about true dreams and visions.

## True dreams and visions expose sin and produce repentance

While the false prophets may tell tales of gold dust and rainbows, a dream from the Most High will cause an awareness of sin, and a desperation to make things right. When the modern day prophets tell us of their dreams and visions, does it cause us to drop to our knees in sorrow and humbly repent?

## True dreams and visions give you His peace without creating a worldview based on fantasy.

There is a peace that the believers in China and other "Gospel-hostile" countries experience that is completely different from the "peace" peddled by the false prophets in our Western culture. This peace is not founded on comforting lies that deceive us into believing we will never be hunted for our faith, and that God is going to overlook the sin of our nation. True peace assures us that, if we obey His voice, He will never leave us nor forsake us - even in the midst of tribulation.

## True dreams and visions have value and make you useful to the Kingdom

In the last chapter, our reference verse for this point was **Jeremiah 23:16-17**. Let us take another look, shall we?

> ### Jeremiah 23:16-17
> *Thus says the LORD of hosts: "Do not listen to the words of the prophets who prophesy to you. They make you worthless. They speak a vision of their own heart, not from the mouth of the LORD. They continually say to those who despise Me, 'The LORD has said, "You shall have peace"'; and to everyone who walks according*

*to the dictates of his own heart, they say, 'No evil shall come upon you.'"*

While false dreams and visions will cause us to become complacent (because we are listening to lies) the true ones will stir in us a longing to be rid of things that have no purpose in His Kingdom. As we purge ourselves, we become honorable vessels, ready for the Master's use **(2 Timothy 2:20-21)**.

## True dreams and visions reveal the True Nature of God

In the last chapter, we took a brief look at Baal, a god who basically "morphed" to fit the views and requirements of the local worshipers.

The modern day church has its own images of Baal that it worships. These images (which they call "Jesus" and/or "God") adapt and change to fit the needs and expectations of the people as time progresses, just like Baal did.

Does that sound too far out? Ask yourself:

- *Does my god have 44,000 versions of the truth? (FYI: There are over 44,000 Christian denominations in existence today)*

- *Does my god accept unrepentant homosexuals?*

- *Does my god teach that it's ok to embrace pagan festivals and practices?*

- *Does my god reward me according to my deeds or my intent?*

- *Does my god believe Israel is not entitled to the full scope of the Promised Land?*

- *Does my god change in any way?*

Baal would probably do all of the above. The God of the Bible doesn't.

Rather than paint an image of God that fits the whims of the people, a true dream or vision will always agree with His Divine Word.

OK, so now that we have derived the characteristics of God-ordained dreams and visions from what the Word says about the false, let us analyze real life examples of "prophetic" dreams and visions, using the information that we have learned.

## BOBBY CONNER'S DREAM ABOUT BOB JONES

Even though the Word prohibits contact with the dead, people in the prophetic movement claim that, through dreams, visions and occasionally physical encounters, they (as well as you) can speak with deceased prophets, mentors and other "spiritual giants" from yesteryear. Apparently, what was once an abomination in the eyes of God is now an acceptable method of communication.

In an Elijah List article from 2014, Bobby Conner reported having a dream where he met with the late Bob Jones.

In spite of the fact that Mr. Jones' prophetic record is filled with holes, his scriptural interpretation corrupted (to put it lightly), and his ministry tainted with sexual scandal,[1] the prophetic movement and its false prophets warmly embrace the dearly departed as a "spiritual father" and "beloved prophetic leader."[2]

> *Turning to look at my windows, suddenly with a flash of light appearing just outside my window, striding down what appeared to be translucent, pearl-colored stairs, was Bob Jones. He had the most winsome, warm smile*

*and looked absolutely wonderful. However, in the dream I was completely aware that Bob had passed and gone to Heaven on February 14, 2014.*

*Bob simply stepped into my study. I did not need to open the window, he just walked right in. His appearance was incredible: He was firm and fit, and he was dressed in a wonderful, soft, beautiful, elegant, white robe past his waist down below his knees, like a long shirt. His hair was extremely white and glistening. I was amazed at his skin: It was without blemish, white and soft, and his smile was truly radiant and beautiful. His eyes were bigger than normal and extremely clear, sparkling like that of an excited child.* [2]

From the onset of this account, Bobby Conner is quick to paint a "heavenly" image of Bob Jones, complete with a flash of light, white robe, glistening skin and white hair. No doubt, this pseudo-messianic description served to dazzle the Elijah List faithful and prophetic community worldwide.

Bobby Conner, who is endorsed as a true prophet and father in the prophetic, further builds upon this deception by glamorizing necromancy,[3] telling his listeners that he, as a "father" in the prophetic, looked forward to encounters with the deceased, and apparently the feeling is mutual!

*I had been expecting his visit; nevertheless, words can't describe my delight and thrill! I was so excited to see my dear friend, I said, "I've been expecting this meeting! And looking forward to it." He quickly replied in an excited tone, "Me too!" His next words were, "You are doing fine!" And he said, placing both hands on his chest, "And I am doing wonderful."* [2]

Bob Jones died on February 14, 2014 and the Elijah List article is dated April 23, 2014. Apparently, the late Bob Jones' couldn't wait 3 months to return from the dead to show Bobby Conner something. Which begs the question:

*What message could be so important that God would violate His own Word and send a mere mortal back to the realm of the living?*

He didn't. This appears to be nothing more than a shameless attempt to use Bob Jones' death and a demonically-inspired dream to elevate Bobby Conner, the Elijah List and the prophetic movement (in general) in the eyes of its adherents. Here is the crux of the message relayed to Bobby Conner by a spirit that called itself "Bob Jones."

The End-Time Harvest is going to be announced and spearheaded by... none other than the prophetic movement!

> *Bob said with a childlike smile, "YOU know what this means don't you?" I replied somewhat tentatively, "I think I do!" He said in a most confident tone, "It is the HARVEST!" He said, "The coming harvest will be spearheaded by the prophetic."*
>
> *The prophets will be used in an unprecedented way to announce and declare the fields that are now ripe and ready for harvest. The prophetic voices will sound a clear trumpet call to bring forth the Body of Christ to stand up and speak up, becoming anointed evangelists.*
>
> *Bob said, almost in a personal matter-of-fact manner, "It is so much better to watch from my vantage point." He added, "I know we have much to talk about, but we will do that later!" And suddenly there was a strong flash of light extremely blue bright, and he was gone. In the*

*dream, I am standing in my study, my body and mind both pulsating, shaken to the core by the visitation.*

Was this dream just a total lie? I don't think so. In my opinion, it probably did occur. Anything at all can happen in your dreams, but it's what you do with those dreams that tells what kind of person you are.

Unfortunately for the unquestioning prophetic masses, this dream was not weighed against scripture and treated accordingly. It was used to further the agenda of an erroneous movement, carelessly distributed around the world and accepted as gospel truth by many.

And, while the false prophets line their pockets, their readers will be pursuing an encounter with the dead. It's all monkey see, monkey do.

> **Jeremiah 23:32**
> *"Behold, I am against those who prophesy false dreams," says the LORD, "and tell them, and cause My people to err by their lies and by their recklessness. Yet I did not send them or command them; therefore they shall not profit this people at all," says the LORD.*

It's a sad truth that the false prophets will go to great lengths to see to it that they stay in the limelight, even if it means deceiving the masses and capitalizing on a friend's death.

Wolves indeed.

## LET'S APPLY WHAT WE'VE LEARNED TO BOBBY CONNER'S VISION

I'm going to grit my teeth hard and overlook the fact that Mr. Conner is talking to a dead person. Let's say (just for the sake of argument) that God is alright with necromancy. Does Bobby's dream of the late Bob Jones do any of the following?

- *Stir you to repent?*

- *Give you the assurance that God is with you in the midst of tribulation if you obey Him?*

- *Stir in you a desire to rid yourself of anything that hinders your usefulness to the Kingdom?*

- *Paint an accurate, scriptural picture of God/Jesus?*

I think you have your answer.

## PAUL CAIN AND HIS FALSE VISION OF THE ANGEL OF THE LORD

When the Lakeland Revival was occurring in Florida, controversially "restored" homosexual and alcoholic Paul Cain[6] (false prophet) claims to have heard a message from the Angel of the Lord in regard to Todd Bentley.

> *"I thank you that you have answered my prayer that you have let me live to see tokens of this revival and be involved in it in some way or a participant if possible ... and Lord, You have never allowed me to say that I have met the New Breed ... Absolutely met the New Breed! And when you brought Todd Bentley and I together, the angel of the Lord said 'you have found what you are looking for,' ... this is a man without guile ... behold Nathaniel in whom there is no guile! ... I've stood by the notables and the greats that had the greatest healing ministry of all times and I've never met anyone that has the integrity and the possibilities of leading this thing into a worldwide revival. And I just want to confer and bless ... whatever I can do, ... I just place to myself to*

*hear from the Lord and to transfer and to give to my brother who has given so much to others and soo much to me, everything you have ever deposited into my life that I didn't know how to give away I'm giving it to my brother tonight to carry on this revival until the stadiums all over the world have been, uh … catching this, have been carriers of it and taking it from one end of the world to the other and thank you I'VE MET THE NEW BREED TONIGHT."* [4]

Well, apparently that didn't work out. Paul Cain's prophecy was proven false when, within a very, very short period of time, it was revealed that Todd Bentley had an "inappropriate relationship" with another woman. Do you think Nathaniel, *"a man in whom is no guile"* would do something like that?

In spite of Bentley's antics, his fans didn't have long to wait, because Rick Joyner and other false prophets immediately came to the rescue and had him "restored" within a year (give or take a few months) with new wife in tow, of course.

OK, I'm going to grit my teeth again, but let's say (just for the sake of argument) that God is fine with a "restored" alcoholic sodomite passing his mantle to a man hovering dangerously close to the sin of adultery. Does Paul Cain's vision of the "Angel of the Lord" do any of the following?

- *Stir you to repent?*

- *Give you the assurance that God is with you in the midst of tribulation if you obey Him?*

- *Stir in you a desire to rid yourself of anything that hinders your usefulness to the Kingdom?*

- *Paint an accurate, scriptural picture of God/Jesus?*

Do you see how obvious this is?

I think you have your answer as to whether Paul Cain REALLY saw the Angel of the Lord.

## PROPHESYING FALSE DREAMS AND VISIONS IS WITCHCRAFT

With the examples provided in this book, you should see a very close connection between false prophets and sorcery/witchcraft/soothsaying. But let us look to the Word for something more direct. The act of carelessly prophesying a false vision is actually EQUATED with witchcraft.

> **Jeremiah 14:14-15**
> *And the LORD said to me, "The prophets prophesy lies in My name. I have not sent them, commanded them, nor spoken to them; they prophesy to you a false vision, divination [qecem – H7081][5], a worthless thing, and the deceit of their heart." Therefore thus says the LORD concerning the prophets who prophesy in My name, whom I did not send, and who say, "Sword and famine shall not be in this land" – "By sword and famine those prophets shall be consumed!"*

From the Scripture above, we can easily see that prophesying a false vision IS divination. In fact, this is the SAME WORD that Samuel used when he rebuked Saul.

> **1 Samuel 15:23**
> *For rebellion is as the sin of witchcraft [qecem – H7081][5], and stubbornness is as iniquity and idolatry. Because thou hast rejected the word of the LORD, he hath also rejected thee from being king.*

Thus we can safely arrive at the following conclusion:

## PROPHESYING A FALSE VISION =

## REBELLION =

## WITCHCRAFT

It couldn't be any clearer. The people who prophesy of "heavenly visions" that do not line up with what GOD says in His Word are performing outright witchcraft. And I don't think that I would be too far off-the-mark to say that, in God's eyes, the prophesying of false dreams is just as offensive.

This is why it is SO important for us to learn how to discern between the Holy and profane when it comes to dreams and visions.

When the Messiah returns, those who are careless in their discernment will find themselves in the same lot as those who practice witchcraft. I definitely do not want to be numbered with them. How about you?

**Footnotes:**

[1] Olathe Daily News (11/13/91 – "Minister removed after confession of sexual misconduct"

[2] ElijahList.com (04/23/14) - "Bobby Conner: Golden Shafts - It's About the Harvest! A Dream Visitation From Bob Jones" Link: http://www.elijahlist.com/words/display_word.html?ID=13358

[3] Necromancy - the supposed practice of communicating with the dead, especially in order to predict the future.

[4] YouTube video: "Self-restored homosexual Paul Cain transfers his deviant anointing to Todd Bentley": https://youtu.be/dqOUsjLloZs

[5] Blueletter Bible definition of the word "qecem" [H7081] https://www.blueletterbible.org/lang/lexicon/lexicon.cfm?Strongs=H7081&t=KJV

[6] Prophetic Minister Paul Cain Issues Public Apology for Immoral Lifestyle http://www.charismamag.com/site-archives/154-peopleevents/people-and-events/1514-prophetic-minister-paul-cain-issues-public-apology-for-immoral-lifestyle-

# SCRIPTURAL WITNESS #7: FALSE PROPHETS ALWAYS HAVE AN ENCOURAGING WORD

Before you start reading this next chapter, I must give this small caveat.

*I believe that the demonstration of God's love and compassion is a vital function of the Body of Christ. God is overjoyed when we comfort and show affection to the broken, give encouragement to the downcast and give sustenance to the needy. As His ambassadors, we must be faithful in all of these areas!*

*But this is not the ministry or function of the prophet!*

*The goal of this book is to show you how to use Scripture to recognize a false prophet. And the overemphasis on being "positive and encouraging" is part of the masquerade. So, while I seem to be less-than-enthusiastic about a false prophet's need to "gush" over sinners, please do not take this as a sign that I believe we are to be harsh with our words all the time.*

*There is a time and a place for everything, but I believe the aforementioned overemphasis on the "positive" is ill-timed and misplaced.*

## FALSE PROPHETS AND WILLFUL BLINDNESS

There is an enchanting mindset that has taken root in the church that is causing everyone to turn a blind eye to sin.

According to the current trend, you are not allowed to discuss sin, expose sin or (God forbid) correct sin, otherwise you are perceived as "not walking in love" and branded as immature, hateful, legalistic, or somehow ignorant of God's grace.

However, if you ignore (or marginalize) sin and its penalty, speak only positive and encouraging words, and preach a licentious, unscriptural approach to grace, then you are esteemed as someone worthy of acceptance and adoration. This ecclesiastical form of political correctness plays right into the ethos of a false prophet.

The following quote from a well-known prophetic ministry is a great summation of a false prophet's view towards delivering a prophecy.

*The very essence of the prophetic gift is more about encouragement than rebuke and causing others to see into their future. This promotes THANKSGIVING for what it's shown. Some exhortation or rebuke or warning is sometimes part of the prophetic but mostly, it's encouragement!* [1]

## THE FALSE PROPHET - SINFUL PEOPLE DYNAMIC

The relationship between a false prophet and a sinful nation hasn't changed in over 2,000 years. Sinful people instruct the prophet to speak what they want to hear.

### Isaiah 30:9-10
*That this is a rebellious people, lying children, <u>children who will not hear the law of the LORD</u>; Who say to the seers, <u>"Do not see," and to the prophets, "Do not prophesy to us right things; speak to us smooth things, prophesy deceits."</u>*

As a result of this pressure, the false prophets lie, saying *"You shall have peace"* when there is no peace.

**Jeremiah 6:14**
*They have healed also the hurt of the daughter of my people slightly, <u>saying, "Peace, peace;" when there is no peace</u>.*

As stated in a previous chapter, *"the hurt"* being addressed here is the broken covenant between God and His people, Israel. It is the same today. Iniquity continues to be ignored by the false prophets who will speak only the *"smooth things"* and *"deceits"* demanded by their worshipers. The false prophets (and their devotees) try to put a positive spin on it by saying they are "being positive and encouraging," or "promoting unity in the Body," or "showing the Love of God," but God calls it healing the hurt *"slightly"* [qalal – H7043][2] which, according to the *Strong's concordance* entry, means to <u>treat the sin as something that is of no consequence</u>.

Even though the false prophet and the sinful nation both know in their hearts that sin is a factor that needs to be addressed, they ignore God's warning that *"the wages of sin is death"* and continue on their pathway in ignorant, deceptive bliss. Thus the deceivers and the deceived share the mutually deserved repercussion.

## FALSE PROPHETS IGNORE THEIR DUTY TO DECLARE SIN TO THE BODY

Do you remember the foundational pillars of our faith that we discussed in **Scriptural Witness #4**? If not, you may want to review them before continuing with this chapter.

Our unchangeable God did not change between the Old and New Testaments. If God did not change, then the message of His prophets did not change either. The goal has always been the same - to call His people back to obedience to His commandments, so that they could be blessed.

This is even backed up by Scripture in the New Testament. **1 Corinthians 14** (the "go to" chapter for the modern day prophetic movement) says:

> **1 Corinthians 14:22**
> *So you see that speaking in tongues is a sign, not for believers, but for unbelievers. <u>Prophecy, however, is for the benefit of believers</u>, not unbelievers.*

> **1 Corinthians 14:24-25**
> *But <u>if all of you are prophesying</u>, and unbelievers or people who don't understand these things come into your meeting, <u>they will be convicted of sin and judged by what you say</u>. As they listen, their secret thoughts will be exposed, and they will fall to their knees and worship God, declaring, "God is truly here among you."*

Contrary to what the false prophets say, prophecy is all about correction and purging sin out of the life of the believer. Encouragement only comes into the picture when sin is repented of and true righteousness is lived out. This is a pattern that can be seen in both the Old and New Testaments.

Regardless of the "dispensation," prophets judged sin on a regular basis. From Elijah pronouncing judgment upon Ahab and Jezebel **(1 Kings 21:20-24)** to Peter pronouncing judgment upon the wickedness of Ananias and Sapphira **(Acts 5)**, the proclamation of judgment upon sin has always been a central duty of God's prophets.

**BEFORE YOU CONTINUE:** If you're still convinced that guidelines for Old Testament prophecy and New Testament prophecy are different, please refer to **Appendix C**, where I have included my article *"New Testament Prophecy – Understanding 1 Corinthians 14."* In this article, I go into greater detail on **1 Corinthians 14**, one of the most misunderstood chapters in the Bible.

## FALSE PROPHETS SUPPORT AND ENCOURAGE
## THOSE WHO LIVE SINFUL LIVES

In the same way that true disciples find comfort in the words of the true prophets, people who pursue fleshly desires will find comfort and affirmation in a false prophet's words. This is the way it has always been. It was true in the Old Testament **(1 Kings 22:8)**, it was true in the New Testament **(Luke 6:26, Acts 8:9-11, 13: 4-12, 1 John 4:1)** and it is true today **(2 Peter 2:3, 18)**. The deceived find themselves drawn to the positive and encouraging words, doled out freely by the false prophets, who will tell them exactly what they want to hear, regardless of where they are in their walks with God.

This reckless approach to prophetic ministry does not heal; instead, it causes the hearers to become complacent. The perception is that if God has nothing but complimentary and supportive things to say to the hearers while they are wallowing in the mire of their sin, then there is no need to repent.

### Jeremiah 23:14
*Also I have seen a horrible thing in the prophets of Jerusalem: They commit adultery and walk in lies; They also strengthen the hands of evildoers, So that no one turns back from his wickedness. All of them are like Sodom to Me, and her inhabitants like Gomorrah.*

To *"strengthen the hands"* of a person means to reinforce and augment (either by verbal support or physical assistance) whatever behavior or actions that person is already doing.

### DON'T BE AN AHAB

Ahab is noted for being the Kingdom of Israel's most wicked king. Let's just face it, you can't get any worse than having "married Jezebel" on your permanent record!

**1 Kings 16:30**

*And Ahab the son of Omri did evil in the sight of the LORD above all that were before him.*

Still, even in the midst of Ahab's extreme wickedness and disregard for the God of Abraham, Isaac and Jacob, the false prophets insisted on speaking positive and encouraging words to him. While considering this, remember, the false prophets were *convinced* that they were doing the right thing! As far as we know, NOT ONE of them had a malicious intent to deceive the king and bring about his demise.

**1 Kings 22:6**

*Then the king of Israel gathered the prophets together, about four hundred men, and said to them, "Shall I go against Ramoth Gilead to fight, or shall I refrain?" So they said, "Go up, for the Lord will deliver [it] into the hand of the king."*

**1 Kings 22:11**

*Now Zedekiah the son of Chenaanah had made horns of iron for himself; and he said, "Thus says the LORD: 'With these you shall gore the Syrians until they are destroyed.'" And all the prophets prophesied so, saying, "Go up to Ramoth Gilead and prosper, for the LORD will deliver [it] into the king's hand."*

Even after a true prophet, Micaiah, spoke a real word from God to King Ahab, Ahab chose to heed the false prophet's words instead of the true. Apparently, the positive and encouraging report was preferable to the rebuke.

But he paid for that error with his life.

## WHEN THE HEART IS LED ASTRAY

There is not one person in the prophetic church who will profess to despise God. They are convinced that their verbal adoration, altruistic deeds and "extravagant worship" demonstrate that their hearts are in the right place. But according the Word of God, their disobedience to His commandments and their adoration of man-made doctrines reveals that their hearts have actually been led astray.

The Father spoke of them long ago.

**Isaiah 29:13-14**
*Therefore the Lord said: "<u>Inasmuch as these people draw near with their mouths and honor Me with their lips</u>, but have removed their hearts far from Me, and <u>their fear toward Me is taught by the commandment of men</u>, Therefore, behold, I will again do a marvelous work among this people, a marvelous work and a wonder; <u>for the wisdom of their wise men shall perish, and the understanding of their prudent men shall be hidden</u>."*

**Psalm 119:67**
*Before I was afflicted <u>I went astray</u>: but now have <u>I kept thy word</u>.*

**Amos 2:4**
*Thus says the LORD: "For three transgressions of Judah, and for four, I will not turn away its punishment, <u>because they have despised the law of the LORD, and have not kept His commandments. Their lies lead them astray, lies which their fathers followed</u>."*

**1 John 5:2-3**
*<u>By this we know that we love the children of God</u>, when we love God and keep His commandments. <u>For this is</u>*

*the love of God, that we keep His commandments. And His commandments are not burdensome.*

Make no mistake about it - people who do not follow the commandments of the Most High do not truly love Him, and will follow the dictates of their own hearts (their own relative doctrines) every time. This is why false prophets are drawn to the prophetic movement like flies to road kill - because they virtually ignore the preaching of repentance and relegate His commandments to Old Covenant triviality.

## WHY REBUKE A MAN WHEN YOU CAN GIVE HIM A GOOD SCRATCH INSTEAD?

False prophets will never address sin directly, unless it is sin against them or their ministries. Any other statements regarding sin are ambiguous, at best. Some even go so far as to embrace sin, renaming it "freedom."

The false prophets know that taking a stand for righteousness, which would draw people back to the commandments of God, would inevitably cost them disciples and hit them hard in their pocketbooks. The most grievous offenses get overlooked because of this weak-kneed approach to what God hates.

The path of least resistance is always the preferred approach. So instead of getting right with the Most High, the crowds get entertained with anecdotes of dreams, visions and miracles that may (or may not) have occurred. If that doesn't work, the speaker will share a perverted message of God's love and grace, applying a soothing scratch to the itching ear.

## WHEN SPEAKING TRUTH BECOMES A SIN

As I mentioned above, false prophets will believe correction is in order when they or their ministries, are being questioned.

This dynamic is extremely frustrating. I've seen sins like adultery, homosexuality and murder[3] get glossed over, but the supposed sin of comparing a false prophet's words or decisions to the Word of God seems to cross the proverbial line in the sand. Prepare to be demonized if you dare to step over that line.

False prophets see those who weigh their words against Scripture, and dare to speak out about it as divisive, legalistic and judgmental. In the minds of these counterfeits, those who behave as true Bereans are people trapped by a "religious" or "legalistic" spirit (both phrases you will never find in the Bible), who really need to get a better revelation of God's grace.

Life would be much easier for them if you would be silent, supportive and willfully-ignorant like the rest of their followers, who trust them implicitly to give the undiluted prophetic word. They may clothe their defense in pleasant words, but if you read between the lines, you can hear them say, "Just shut up and agree with what I'm saying and doing."

The Word of God, however, says something different:

### Jeremiah 23:16-17
*Thus says the LORD of hosts: "Do not listen to the words of the prophets who prophesy to you. They make you worthless; They speak a vision of their own heart, Not from the mouth of the LORD. They continually say to those who despise Me, 'The LORD has said, "You shall have peace"'; And [to] everyone who walks according to the dictates of his own heart, they say, 'No evil shall come upon you.'"*

## FALSE PROPHETS REFUSE TO DECLARE SIN TO A SINFUL NATION

A false prophet's philosophy in addressing the sin of an individual also carries over in his/her prophetic words to a nation. Since the prophet is God's spokesman, and God must judge sin in order to be a Righteous Judge, declaring the sin of a nation (or a people group) should be a natural function of the prophetic ministry, but such is not the case with our current mainstream prophetic celebrities.

Like the false prophets of old, our current charlatans refuse to believe that God will judge their sin or the sin of the nation they are sent to. Regardless of the state of their nations in relation to righteousness, they will always find something flattering to say, because they know that itching ears are a given in every congregation. People are interested more in feeling better about themselves than in repenting of their sins. False prophets in the United States and Canada are particularly guilty of this misrepresentation of God. According to Scripture, they have "become wind" and God refuses to put His Word in their mouths.

As these imposters prophesy great and wonderful things for our continent, they willfully ignore the truth that God must judge our nation according to His Word, and that doesn't necessarily mean we will have to wait until Judgment Day for it to happen. Just ask Sodom, Gomorrah, Tyre, Pompeii and other countries that have felt a measure of God's judgment...

Oh, wait a minute, they're no longer here to ask.

These days, if a prophet prophesies anything but peace for the United States (or North America in general), he/she is branded a "doom and gloom prophet" and ignored by the majority.

### Jeremiah 5:11-13

*"For the house of Israel and the house of Judah Have dealt very treacherously with Me," says the LORD. They have lied about the LORD, And said, "[It is] not He. Neither will evil come upon us, Nor shall we see sword or famine. And the prophets become wind, For the word [is] not in them." Thus shall it be done to them.*

### Jeremiah 14:13-15

*Then I said, "Ah, Lord GOD! Behold, the prophets say to them, 'You shall not see the sword, nor shall you have famine, but I will give you assured peace in this place.' And the LORD said to me, "The prophets prophesy lies in My name. I have not sent them, commanded them, nor spoken to them; they prophesy to you a false vision, divination* **(remember, this means 'witchcraft'),** *a worthless thing, and the deceit of their heart." Therefore thus says the LORD concerning the prophets who prophesy in My name, whom I did not send, and who say, "Sword and famine shall not be in this land" – "By sword and famine those prophets shall be consumed!"*

## BUT THE UNITED STATES SUPPORTS ISRAEL!

False prophets and the church in America look at our relationship with Israel as a safety net. Somehow, because we have given political, military and financial support to Israel, we believe that this will excuse our many sins in the eyes of God. At the very least, we are deluded into thinking that it will increase His tolerance for our abominations.

Let me give you some news (and this is going to be a bitter pill to swallow).

The United States has only supported (and will only support) Israel as long as it benefits us financially, politically and militarily. At the same time, Israel will only support the United States as long as we support them militarily, diplomatically, etc.

I'm sure that there are other relational factors that I haven't considered, but the point is that both countries are in this relationship for no other reason than mutual gain. Israel doesn't love the United States unconditionally, nor does the U.S. love Israel because of some "spiritual mandate."

I'm not saying that there isn't anyone in our government who loves Israel with a God-influenced love. What I'm saying is that the prevailing motive behind the relationship between our countries is greed, not covenant.

Was that tough to acknowledge? Well, I'm going to take this just a little further.

For the most part, the Western church will only love Israel as long as it benefits them. We love to take the promises meant for Israel and apply them to us when it benefits us, heartily claiming *"there is no Jew or Gentile in Christ Jesus!"* But whenever something is required of us, like obedience to God's commands, we vehemently shout, *"That's only for the Jews!!!"*

What hypocrisy.

Building upon this deception, false prophets will zealously declare our love for Israel and the perceived benefits of that relationship, comforting the masses with a false peace. Subconsciously, the people in the pew think, *"Well, if prophet so-and-so says it's true, then it must be true!"* But if we open our eyes, we can see that reality is saying something entirely different.

There is no love - or loyalty - in our relationship with Israel.

This dynamic is evident in our government today. Because Israel is no longer perceived as an asset, and because our current president's allegiance is to another agenda entirely, those in the administration and most of the country are turning their backs on Israel, leaving them as food for the wolves. Because our government will not keep their promise to assist Israel, Israel no longer trusts us as friends.

The false prophets simply cannot fathom this, because it contradicts their deception.

## FALSE PROPHETS DECLARE "GOD IS ON OUR SIDE!" WHILE THEY DIVINE FOR MONEY

What we've discussed in this chapter is actually a repetition of history. In the book of Micah, the false prophets would give false assurance to their audiences, telling them things that they wanted to hear, but demonizing those who wouldn't buy into their shenanigans.

### Micah 3:5
*Thus says the LORD concerning the prophets who make my people stray; <u>who chant "Peace" while they chew with their teeth</u>, but <u>who prepare war against him who puts nothing into their mouths</u>:*

The false prophets would also *"divine for money,"* all the while declaring that no harm would come to the nation of Israel because God was on their side.

### Micah 3:11-12
*Her heads judge for a bribe, her priests teach for pay, <u>and her prophets divine for money</u>. Yet they lean on the LORD, and say, "Is not the LORD among us? No harm can come upon us." Therefore <u>because of you</u> Zion shall be plowed like a field, Jerusalem shall become heaps of*

*ruins, and the mountain of the temple like the bare hills of the forest.*

God, speaking through Micah, conveyed that Zion would be brought to ruin and the blame would be placed squarely on the prophets' (as well as the leaders' and priests') shoulders.

## WHY WOULD THE PROPHETS BE TO BLAME?

The Word of God says in many places that the cause of Israel's destruction was their idolatry. But in the book of Micah, it says that it is because of the prophets that *"Zion shall be plowed like a field, Jerusalem shall become heaps of ruins, and the mountain of the temple like the bare hills of the forest."*

Why is God saying now that it is the prophets' fault?

Because the prophets weren't *speaking* what they were told to speak. These imposters had the gift of prophecy and they should have been faithfully speaking God's message to His people, not flattering them in their decadence.

Remember the message of the prophets that we read about in Chapter 4?

> *"God is returning to set up His Kingdom! Repent from your wicked ways and return to His Ways! Obey His commands... all of them! If you do, GOOD things will happen! If you refuse, BAD things will happen!"*

The prophets in Micah's time were not speaking that message. They were too preoccupied with speaking positive and encouraging words that scratched the itching ears of the ignorant masses. Just like the prophetic church today, the listeners would be assured that God was on their side and no harm would come to them. Since the message of repentance was not preached, *the need* for repentance was never understood. Thus the people would perish in their sin because the prophets had *"become wind."*

History does indeed repeat itself.

## THE MARK OF A FAITHFUL PROPHET

After denouncing the false prophets of Israel, Micah declared his own faithfulness to the task that God had set before him.

> **Micah 3:8**
> *But truly I am full of power by the Spirit of the LORD, and of justice and might, to declare to Jacob his transgression and to Israel his sin.*

In the midst of the political correctness of his day, Micah refused to bow to the pressure of his fellow prophets. He spoke the undiluted Word of the Lord and remained true to the true prophets' message.

Where can we find this today in the prophetic movement?

## THE PUNISHMENT OF A DECEIVED PROPHET

As I've studied the Word of God, my view towards the false prophet issue has changed. I used to view this matter as "good prophet vs. bad prophet." Now I realize that this is inaccurate; it is more like "true prophet vs. deceived prophet."

With the exception of Balaam, I cannot find anywhere in the Word of God where it says that false prophets were scheming to bring about the destruction of Israel. The Word never says that they wanted to see their country fall into the hands of the Babylonians, Assyrians or any foreign army.

No, these false prophets had good (yet very misguided) intentions toward their nation. They were a deceived group of people who had the gift of prophecy, but they led the masses astray by that gift. They thought that they could use that gift to speak positive and encouraging words to their listeners, and maybe make a little cash on the side, but instead their words were used by the enemy to lull the nation to sleep.

The prophet Micah speaks of their punishment.

> **Micah 3:6-7**
> *Therefore you shall have night without vision, and you shall have darkness without divination; the sun shall go down on the prophets, and the day shall be dark for them. So the seers shall be ashamed, and the diviners abashed; indeed they shall all cover their lips; for there is no answer from God.*

God spoke of a time when there would be *"night without vision"* for these prophets... *"darkness without divination."* In the day of God's judgment upon the nation of Israel, the *"sun would go down"* and the *"day would be dark"* for them. As the realization that they had led the people astray sank in, they would be so ashamed that they would *"cover their lips,"* which is closely associated with leprosy **(Leviticus 13:45)** as well as being a mark of shame.

They will wonder *"What happened? Where is the Word of the Lord?"*

History is going to repeat itself, and God will judge the sins of America, Canada and the rest of the world. Our current false prophets will be perplexed and dismayed at what they see happening around them. They will be confused and troubled because they were convinced that God was telling them to stay positive and encouraging in their ministry - even to people wallowing in their sin.

They sought for healing and kindness, but instead, they destroyed nations.

They will question, *"Is the Lord not faithful to His Word?"*

And the Conquering King will answer…. **"I AM."**

**Footnotes:**

[1] ElijahList.com (11/24/2011) - "Steve Shultz: Thanksgiving at the White House(s)"
Link: http://www.elijahlist.com/words/display_word.html?ID=10477

[2]  Blueletter Bible definition of the word "qalal" [H7043]
https://www.blueletterbible.org/lang/lexicon/lexicon.cfm?strongs=H7043&t=KJV

[3]  Huffington Post article: "Cult Murder Case Involving 'Ex-Gay' Leader Puts Spotlight on Radical Prayer Center"
Link: http://www.huffingtonpost.com/wayne-besen/
cult-murder-puts-spotlight-on-radical-prayer-center_b_2161510.html

# SCRIPTURAL WITNESS #8: FALSE PROPHETS WON'T HAVE AN ORIGINAL THOUGHT

From what I've written so far, a clearer image of the false prophet should be forming in your mind. In fact, you should see each Scriptural witness set forth in this series overlapping or connecting with the others, like pieces in a giant puzzle. We have 3 more pieces to go, in order complete this puzzle, so let's keep going!

## SATAN AND HIS DISCIPLES CANNOT CREATE ANYTHING

No matter how badly he wants to, Satan cannot create anything because he is not the Creator. Satan can only take what has already been created and twist it for his own evil, selfish purposes. His servants are no different.

### 2 Corinthians 11:12-15

*But what I do, I will also continue to do, that I may cut off the opportunity from <u>those who desire an opportunity to be regarded just as we are</u> in the things of which they boast. For such are false apostles, deceitful workers, <u>transforming themselves into apostles of Christ</u>.*

*And no wonder! For Satan himself transforms himself into an angel of light. <u>Therefore it is no great thing if his ministers also transform themselves into ministers of</u>*

*righteousness, whose end will be according to their works.*

Taking on the nature of their father, the false prophets will arrogantly claim to be enlightened ministers of the Gospel. They want you to think that they are people who have tapped into the spiritual resources of the heavenly realm, but no matter how hard they try, authentic prophecy always seems elude them.

To compensate for this lack of authenticity, these imposters will:

- *Take what our Father says and pervert it;*

- *Repeat what has been prophesied before;*

- *Take a prior false prophet's prophecy and twist it further.*

Usually, you will find the latter 2 to be the most common.

In the earlier days of the prophetic movement, the "prophetic forerunners" like Bob Jones, Paul Cain, and Mike Bickle would take the Word of God and twist it to fit their own agendas. Presently, the children of the movement will hang on every word that pours forth from their mouths as **IF** it were the Word of God and read the Word of God (if they read the Word at all) through their "father's" perverted lens. They only **SEE** what they've been instructed to **SEE** and **UNDERSTAND** what they've been instructed to **UNDERSTAND**.

All critical thinking has been tossed out the door.

Like the forerunners of the 80's and 90's, present day false prophets take advantage of this gullibility and ignorance in their followers to further their own ministries as well as the agenda of the prophetic movement. Most of the younger prophets have no idea that they are doing this; they are merely following the business/ministry model that they have been shown by those who have gone before. Convinced that they have special inroads into the Father's presence and are doing the Father's work, they do not realize that they are taking on the mantle of the Pharisees.

Jesus, speaking to the Pharisees, said:

> **John 8:44**
> *You are of your father the devil, and the desires of your father you want to do. He was a murderer from the beginning, <u>and does not stand in the truth, because there is no truth in him</u>. When he speaks a lie, he speaks from his own resources, for he is a liar and the father of it.*

What is the Truth that Jesus is referring to?

> **John 17:17**
> *Sanctify them by Your truth. Your word is truth.*

What was considered God's Word before the New Testament was written? The Torah and the Prophets! The very books that the false prophets avoid, unless a couple verses happen to support their ideology.

## PROPHETIC EMPIRES BUILT ON REPETITION

Another way the false prophets take advantage of the ignorance and gullibility of their followers is by methodically repeating each other's twisted and perverted prophecies. These inaccurate and rehashed prophecies are readily absorbed by the listener, who would rather rely on the word of man than the Word of God. This, too, serves to further the prophetic ministry and agenda.

There is a lot of money to be made from selling the "prophetic word from God." You can create your own little mini-empire from it and live comfortably! Because of this, false prophets have no problem taking each other's material, tweaking it to sound just *a little* different, and then promoting it as a new revelation from God. This is done all the time, and the sheeple devour it because:

- *They don't think for themselves.*

- *They don't study the Word of God for themselves.*

   *~ and ~*

- *They love to worship their prophetic idols.*

Yes, "prophetic ADHD" is alive and well in the charismatic church. It is uncanny how the sheeple so easily "forget" that the prophet (or one of his/her comrades) boldly proclaimed an IDENTICAL message just a short time earlier. Is this a willful ignorance? Most of the time, I believe it is.

The key verse in this installment holds some of the strongest language I've read about how God feels about the "business" of reusing each other's false prophecy and putting God's name on it.

> **Jeremiah 23:30-32**
> *"Therefore," says the LORD, "<u>I am against these prophets who steal messages from each other and claim they are from me</u>. I am against these smooth-tongued prophets who say, 'This prophecy is from the LORD!'"*
>
> *I am against these false prophets. Their imaginary dreams are flagrant lies that lead my people into sin. I did not send or appoint them, and they have no message at all for my people. I, the LORD, have spoken!*

From reading the verses above, I can't help but feel like the Father is insulted by a false prophet's lack of ingenuity. And there is no scriptural evidence to suggest that the recycling of prophetic messages became an acceptable practice in the New Testament, either.

*Why do the false prophets find it acceptable to use each others' prophetic words?*

1. **It supports the errant doctrine of the prophetic empire.** – Both the prophetic movement and all the individual ministries benefit from this practice, in the long run. Because they have created (and continue to create) a mindset among their listeners, every time the word is repeated, it reinforces the desired mindset.

2. **It energizes a false prophet's self-deception.** – As we have read in Chapter 1, many of these prophets are genuinely nice people, but they are very deceived. As they hear these words and phrases from what they think is the Spirit of God, somehow it reinforces in their minds the delusion that God is speaking to them. But they are not hearing from God. They are either hearing from a deceiving spirit, or they have just heard that "word" before from someone else. This error occurs because they have not been taught to discern between the Holy Spirit, another spirit, and their own thoughts and opinions.

## DISCERNING PROPHETIC AGREEMENT

While studying this in the Word, a student can quickly find a possible conflict.

Many of the Old Testament prophets agreed with each other, and had almost identical messages for Israel. Knowing that the Father is against people who steal prophetic words from each other, and yet His own prophets appeared to be speaking the same thing, how do we balance that out?

What's the difference between prophetic agreement and stealing? If the modern day prophets are saying the same thing (or virtually the same thing) as each other, is it God confirming His Word? Or should we assume that they are just deceived people agreeing over error, and ignore it?

As I mentioned in chapter 3, **Deuteronomy 18:20-22** firmly instructs us that when a prophecy is given and doesn't come to pass, the person who gave it is to be labeled as a false prophet and should be ignored. If a person who is already known as a false prophet by the scriptural criteria is taking it upon him/herself to prophesy words that are eerily similar to those of other prophets, that person's credibility has already been lost because they're a false prophet. They're already walking in error, so we are instructed to ignore them.

But if the person prophesying has not already "fit the bill" as a false prophet, we need to consider the content of the prophecy.

Here are a couple of questions to ask.

**Does the agreed upon prophecy hold true to the core message of the prophet?**

Does the content hold true to the core message of a prophet, or does it distract? Remember the core message of the prophet?

> *God is returning to set up His Kingdom! Repent from your wicked ways and return to His Ways! Obey His commands... all of them! If you do, GOOD things will happen! If you refuse, BAD things will happen!"*

At its core, does the message call people back to the commandments of God, or does it marginalize repentance and bring other concepts to the forefront?

## Does the agreed upon prophecy prophesy peace to a sinful people?

In this book, we've studied many verses that show how a false prophet will preach a soft message to those who really need sharp rebuke.

The false prophets in Ahab's day preached a positive message to a most sinful king **(1 Kings 16:30, 21:25)**. They all agreed together that God was going to prosper the king's campaign against his enemies **(1 Kings 22:12)**. That obviously did not work out so well **(1 Kings 22:35)**, which leads me to my next point.

## Does the agreed upon prophecy come true?

The false prophets agreed that the King was going to have success, when in fact, he died. Their foretelling obviously did not come to pass. In the same way, false prophets will agree upon MANY different points that:

- *Contradict or ignore the message of the prophet;*

- *Preach peace to a sinful people;*

- *Do not come true.*

However, if the prophets are agreeing on a message that embraces the following points, you can rest assured that it is a true prophecy:

- *True prophecy will validate and endorse the core message of the prophet;*

- *True prophecy will preach against the sin of a sinful people;*

- *True prophecy will come true.*

Hopefully, this will help you determine whether or not the agreement between prophecies is God validating His Word, or just a bunch of "prophetic people" agreeing over an erroneous message that sounds good to the itching ear.

## WHAT KINDS OF CATCH PHRASES DO FALSE PROPHETS BORROW FROM ONE ANOTHER?

Modern day false prophets who get a "new revelation from God" usually trumpet a list of similar prophetic terms and catchphrases. Whether or not they've had a dream or vision, or just want to jump back into the limelight, all they have to do is avail themselves of these terms, write something about it and release it to their mailing list and *[BANG]* the masses are focused on them again. Product sales go up and life is "good."

Here is a list of commonly used (and abused) catch phrases and terms that are tossed around whenever a prophet/prophetess wants to be noticed. The list is far from complete, but it should give you a pretty good idea as to what to look for.

- *Open Doors – Open Gates*

- *Creativity*

- *Breakthrough*

- *Revival – Revival Fire*

- *New Season*

- *Realignment – Promotion – Prosperity*

- *Paradigm Shift*

- *Portals*

- *Dreams & Visions*

- *Healing, Signs & Wonders*

Searching the Elijah List or Identity Network web sites for any of the above keywords will show you how often these terms are utilized by the false prophets. Words from the list above are liberally peppered throughout the entire prophetic database. And yet, **there is still this strange lack of fulfillment**. If even 10% of these prophecies would come true, believers would be faring way better than they are today.

## I BELIEVE THAT THE SUPERNATURAL IS REAL

In writing this chapter, I don't want to give the impression that I stand against or don't believe in the phenomena I have listed above. I certainly believe most of them are in the realm of possibility, although there are a few that I am not 100% certain about.

Regardless of how I feel, according to Scripture, these tokens of God's favor are not to be the focus of true prophecy. I am not denying that Ezekiel, Isaiah and others experienced these things, and it is not out of the question that we might experience them as well, but the focus of any prophecy is not the phenomenon, but the message.

*What is the Father saying to us?*

## LIKE SHEEP WITHOUT A SHEPHERD

There is a reason that the enemy distracts from God's Word using recycled "prophetic words" and man-made prophetic slogans.  It is to keep the sheeple in a constant state of flux.  Those who listen to cookie-cutter false prophets and adhere to their false prophecies are always going from one thing to another.  There is no stability.

But this is not God's way.  He has provided commandments/guidelines for us and a way of life that naturally causes us to reflect the stability of His nature.

Contrary to the dispensational doctrine that has been shoved down our throats, our God does not change **(Malachi 3:6)**, and a follower of the Messiah who changes with each passing prophecy (and prophetic fad) cannot hope to reflect the nature of his/her God.

Our walk with God was meant to be simple.  His commandments are simple.  His ways are simple... they were always simple.

### 2 Corinthians 11:3
*But I fear, lest by any means, as the serpent beguiled Eve through his subtlety, so your minds should be corrupted from <u>the simplicity that is in Christ</u>.*

### Deuteronomy 30:11-14
*This command I am giving you today is not too difficult for you to understand, and it is not beyond your reach. It is not kept in heaven, so distant that you must ask, 'Who will go up to heaven and bring it down so we can hear it and obey?' It is not kept beyond the sea, so far away that you must ask, 'Who will cross the sea to bring it to us so we can hear it and obey?' No, the message is*

*very close at hand; <u>it is on your lips and in your heart so that you CAN obey it</u>.*

When Jesus came to this earth, He saw a people who were not living lives of simple obedience to God, but were victims of the false teachings of their time. The prophecy of Jeremiah regarding Israel had come to pass.

### Jeremiah 50:6

*My people have been lost sheep. Their shepherds have led them astray and turned them loose in the mountains. They have lost their way and can't remember how to get back to the sheepfold.*

As He watched them, His heart broke for them. They had no guidance and no stability. Their shepherds were preaching their own doctrines as if they were from God, and the sheeple listened.

Why did they listen? Because that's what they were taught to do.

### Matthew 9:36

*But when he saw the multitudes, he was moved with compassion on them, because they fainted [G1590 – eklyo],*[1] *and were scattered abroad [G4496 – rhipto],*[2] *as sheep having no shepherd.*

The Greek word **"eklyo"** means to **be set free**, *but weak and tired.*

**"Rhipto"** means to be **thrown down**.

This is the fruit of following the ever-changing ways of man **(Ephesians 4:14)**.

The Pharisees, who claimed to follow God, had added hundreds of rules and regulations to something that was intended to be a simple way of living **(Deuteronomy 30:11-14)**. They came together in agreement over this extraneous, unscriptural teaching and ELEVATED it above the Word of God **(Matthew 15:3)**. This is why Jesus came down hard on the Pharisees. They were in agreement over error and were leading the people astray. But, being the Good Shepherd that He is, He came to right that wrong and gather His sheep together.

### Matthew 15:24
*But he answered and said, "I am not sent but unto the lost sheep of the house of Israel."*

### John 11:51-52
*And this spake he not of himself: but being high priest that year, he prophesied that Jesus should die for that nation; and not for that nation only, but that also he should gather together in one the children of God that were scattered abroad.*

How would Jesus gather His sheep together? David, a man after God's own heart, gives us a clue.

### Psalm 119:176
*I have gone astray like a lost sheep; seek thy servant; for I do not forget thy commandments.*

It's the following of His commandments that will gather us *"together in one,"* not joining denominations in order to feed the poor or putting on a city-wide worship service. "Agreeing to disagree" will only accomplish a superficial peace, but will not heal the division between us or bring us into *"unity of the faith."*

The only way to be gathered together as one is to embrace the Kingdom rule by returning to His commandments **(Ecclesiastes 12:13)**. This is never included in a false prophet's message. Rather, he/she will teach you to seek for heavenly encounters and expect paradigm shifts, keeping you unstable and tossed to and fro **(Ephesians 4:14)**.

## BECOMING TRULY "PROPHETIC"

As the false prophets re-use and abuse the Word of God, conforming it to their purposes and augmenting it with their own prophetic catchphrases and tales of supernatural phenomena, the sheep stay confused, wending their way to and fro, thinking that they are free, but still enslaved to their sin.

God explicitly says in His Word that He is against this foolishness.

I want to exhort you, if you haven't opened your eyes yet, DO SO! Don't follow the "group think" of those who ignorantly follow the latest prophetic catchphrases and fads. Return to the Father in repentance and take on His ways by obeying His commandments, discerning between the Holy and the profane.

Then, you will be a *"sign and a wonder"* for those to whom you are sent.

Then, you will truly be "prophetic."

**Footnotes:**

[1] Blueletter bible definition of the word "eklyo" [G1590]
https://www.blueletterbible.org/lang/lexicon/lexicon.cfm?Strongs=G1590&t=N KJV

[2] Blueletter bible definition of the word "rhipto" [G4496]
https://www.blueletterbible.org/lang/lexicon/lexicon.cfm?Strongs=G4496&t=N KJV

# SCRIPTURAL WITNESS #9: FALSE PROPHETS PERFORM MIRACLES, SIGNS AND WONDERS (PART 1)

I firmly believe in a supernatural God who works in the physical realm, performing signs and wonders through those who follow Him. Several people I have known (including my own wife) have had people lay hands on them and experienced healing.

God miraculously intervened in my life by saving me. Not just saving me from the pit, but actually reaching down and pulling me out of circumstances where my life was at risk. He has provided for me supernaturally and delivered me from countless attacks by my enemies (or The Enemy).

I have also experienced the healing power of God first hand, but instead of being on the receiving end of the miracle, I had the privilege of being the vessel He used to heal someone else. This wonderful experience happened when I travelled with Todd Bentley to Uganda.

I actually got to lay my hands on a blind person and watch as God opened his eyes.

Don't mistake that last comment to be an endorsement of Bentley's ministry, or even of my own status with God, for that matter. God will also perform miracles through whomever He chooses - even the disobedient and unfaithful; even outright, evil deceivers.

I know that is hard to fathom for most, but it is still true. Before you label me a heretic, read the rest of this chapter and try to understand where I'm coming from.

## SUPERNATURAL SIGNS AND WONDERS FOLLOW THE BELIEVER

The Word of God states very clearly that miracles, signs and wonders will follow those who follow the Master. Our Messiah said:

### Mark 16:17-18
*<u>And these signs will follow those who believe</u>: In My name they will cast out demons; they will speak with new tongues; they will take up serpents; and if they drink anything deadly, it will by no means hurt them; they will lay hands on the sick, and they will recover.*

After the Messiah rose from the dead, we can see that His words came true.

### Mark 16:20
*And they went out and preached everywhere, the Lord working with them and confirming the word through the accompanying signs. Amen.*

### Acts 6:8
*And Stephen, full of faith and power, did great wonders and signs among the people.*

### Act 8:6
*And the people with one accord gave heed unto those things which Philip spake, hearing and seeing the miracles which he did.*

You can also see this truth in **Acts 8:13, 15:12, 19:11**. All of these verses testify to the reality of the supernatural in the lives of the believers. There should be no doubt about this; the Bible proves it time and time again.

## SIGNS AND WONDERS ARE A MAJOR SIGN OF DECEPTION IN THE LAST DAYS

Nonetheless, the *same* God who wrote all these verses supporting supernatural interaction in the life of the believer also said that miracles, signs and wonders would be a sign of deception in the Last Days!

### Mark 13:22
*For false christs and false prophets will rise and show signs and wonders to deceive, if possible, even the elect.*
**(Also see Matthew 24:24.)**

Paul even speaks of the coming *"lawless one,"* who will use signs and lying wonders to deceive those destined for the pit.

### 2 Thessalonians 2:9-10
*The coming of the lawless one is according to the working of Satan, with all power, signs, and lying wonders, and with all unrighteous deception among those who perish, because they did not receive the love of the truth, that they might be saved.*

So on one side of the coin, we have miracles, signs and wonders following the believer, and on the other side of the coin, we have false prophets using miracles, signs and wonders to deceive. If God performs miracles through His servants, and yet the enemy's servants are doing the exact same thing, we have run into a serious problem.

*How can we discern whether or not these miracles come from the Father? Is it God or satan?*

I'm going to break this topic up into two different chapters. This chapter is going to cover a solid answer based on Scripture. The next chapter will be supplemental information that is open for argument, but I have enough Scripture to back up what I'm going to share, so I believe that there is value in sharing it.

The scriptural evidence in this chapter, however, is indisputable.

## WHEN A SIGN OR A WONDER IS IRRELEVANT

Strangely enough, while the following indisputable points can be found in Scripture, they are rarely considered. God gave us a litmus test for discerning false prophets in the book of Deuteronomy, that is still valid today. This test takes the supernatural phenomena that we are discussing into consideration.

> ### Deuteronomy 13:1-4
> *If there arises among you a prophet or a dreamer of dreams, <u>and he gives you a sign or a wonder</u>, and the sign or the wonder comes to pass, of which he spoke to you, saying, "Let us go after other gods" – which you have not known – "and let us serve them," you shall not listen to the words of that prophet or that dreamer of dreams, for the LORD your God is testing you to know whether you love the LORD your God with all your heart and with all your soul.*
>
> <u>*You shall walk after the LORD your God and fear Him, and keep His commandments and obey His voice; you shall serve Him and hold fast to Him.*</u>

In essence, this scripture is saying that you are to ignore the alleged prophet (or dreamer) if their message causes you to stray from the commandments of God, *<u>even if signs and</u>*

*wonders occur*. These signs and wonders are to have no bearing whatsoever on your discernment. It is all about the prophet's message. Regardless of whether or not he/she is performing signs and wonders, if the prophet is not leading you back to the commandments of the Most High, he/she is to be considered a false prophet.

## SUPERNATURAL SIGNS AND AN ADULTEROUS GENERATION

We have been trained (especially in charismatic circles), to view supernatural activity as a seal of God's approval on a ministry or a person. As a result, people will travel thousands of miles just to experience (or at least view) these signs. But the Master says that an *"evil and adulterous"* generation seeks after a sign.

### Matthew 12:38-39

*Then some of the scribes and Pharisees answered, saying, "Teacher, we want to see a sign from You." But He answered and said to them, "An evil and adulterous generation seeks after a sign…"*

## WHEN MIRACLES, SIGNS AND WONDERS BECOME A TEST FROM GOD

Let's go back again to **Deuteronomy 13:1-4** and take a closer look at it.

### Deuteronomy 13:1-4

*If there arises among you a prophet or a dreamer of dreams, and he gives you a sign or a wonder, and the sign or the wonder comes to pass, of which he spoke to you, saying, "Let us go after other gods" – which you have not known – "and let us serve them," you shall not listen to the words of that prophet or that dreamer of* *dreams, <u>for the LORD your God is testing you</u> to know whether you love the LORD your God with all your heart and with all your soul.*

<u>*You shall walk after the LORD your God and fear Him, and keep His commandments and obey His voice; you shall serve Him and hold fast to Him.*</u>

This verse specifies that, if any supernatural phenomenon occurs, it is a test from God. God Himself is allowing these other-worldly events to occur. It is even possible that God Himself is performing those deeds through the said prophet.

So that could answer the often asked question, *"If I got healed by a false prophet, was it God or the devil?"*

## WHAT ABOUT DEMONIC SIGNS AND WONDERS?

In saying this, I am not omitting the possibility that demonic signs and wonders can occur. They do!

Pharaoh's magicians cast their spells and performed their incantations to mimic a Godly sign. Remember Moses' staff and the rivers turning to blood? Obviously, they were not servants of the Most High, they served the demonic gods of Egypt and were drawing their power from them **(Exodus 7:11, 22)**.

The prophets of baal attempted to invoke the power of their god, even to the point of shedding blood, but they were unsuccessful **(1 Kings 18:26-29)**. But there is no reason to believe that they were not successful before that event.

Having said that, I believe it's entirely possible that the same dynamic could happen today. But we still haven't answered the question: *"How can one be sure that it was God, and not the devil, that produced the signs and wonders?"*

## IF THERE ARISES AMONG YOU A PROPHET...

There seems to be a delineation in Scripture between those who produce miracles through the influence of demonic powers and those who produce signs and wonders by the hand of God. It would seem that the deciding factor was whether or not they were part of Israel.

God told the children of Israel (and us, if we count ourselves among them) in Deuteronomy, *"If there arises AMONG YOU a prophet or a dreamer of dreams."*

It appears that God's testing occurs when a prophet arises from the ranks of the people who name the name of the Most High. This prophet performs signs and wonders, but then steers people away from His commandments.

This type of testing is still happening today in abundance!

## PROPHETS AMONG US – A TRAGEDY

Sadly, it is an all-too-familiar story for many of us.

People who are familiar (our leaders, fathers, mothers, and children) live and grow up among us, attending our churches, worshipping in our congregations and proclaiming the name of Jesus.

At some point, these people experience miracles, divine encounters and other unexplained phenomena. And because the sheeple in our congregations long for the supernatural, the miraculous, or anything outside of this reality, they quickly flock to those who have experienced these signs and wonders, eagerly listening to the wonderful tales of miracles, dreams and heavenly visitations.

Regardless of the spiritual maturity of, or the message preached by, the individual professing these experiences, what usually follows is typical - widespread notoriety, conference speaking engagements and the ever-so-necessary killer web site.

Because all of these wonders occur in the name of Jesus, people automatically assume "That's God!" - and it just might be. But it is God testing us! Will we follow His commands? Or will we be sidetracked by the charismatic celebrity and sideshow phenomena?

Keep in mind **Matthew 12:38-39** and understand that the Greek word for "seeks after" is the word **epizēteō [G1934]**,[1] which means to "wish for, seek diligently for, demand and crave." Let's look at this verse again.

> **Matthew 12:38-39a**
> *Then some of the scribes and Pharisees answered, saying, "Teacher, we want to see a sign from You."*
>
> *But He answered and said to them, "An evil and adulterous generation seeks after [G1934 – epizēteō] a sign ..."*

Does this not perfectly describe the modern day charismatic church?

## MANY WILL COME IN MY NAME, SAYING, "I AM HE"

> **Luke 21:8**
> *And He said: "Take heed that you not be deceived. For many will come in My name, saying, 'I am He,' and, 'The time has drawn near.' Therefore do not go after them."*

The conventional interpretation of this Scripture is that many will come claiming to be the Messiah and deceive many.

Instead of blindly accepting this analysis, we should use our God-given logic and apply it.

*How many people exist on the earth today that claim to be Jesus, the Son of God? How many people have EVER existed who claimed to be Jesus?* Aside from a few nut-jobs - not many.

Jesus said, *"MANY will come in My name...."*

*Did these few loons deceive MANY?* In the grand scheme of things, the deceived were actually very few in number.

How many people are alive today who claim Jesus is the Messiah, but are deceiving multitudes, partially because of the signs and wonders that are being performed? They are too numerous to count.

This is not rocket science, folks. The Messiah forewarned us that the false prophets would rise within our own ranks and proclaim that Yeshua is the Son of God, doing miraculous signs and wonders, and MANY will be deceived.

### 1 John 2:18-19
*Little children, it is the last hour; and as you have heard that the Antichrist is coming, even now many antichrists have come, by which we know that it is the last hour. They went out from us, but they were not of us; for if they had been of us, they would have continued with us; but they went out that they might be made manifest, that none of them were of us.*

### MIRACLES, LAWLESSNESS AND LOVE
### Matthew 24:11-12
*Then many false prophets will rise up and deceive many.*

*And because lawlessness will abound, the love of many will grow cold.*

In these Last Days, we do not want to be among those who allow our love to grow cold. If we do so, we WILL relinquish our "elect" status.

### Mark 13:22
*For false christs and false prophets will rise and show signs and wonders to deceive, if possible, even the elect.*

Friends, I want to exhort you - look at your life! Have you allowed your love to grow cold?

Before you answer that, it is important that you remember to use God's definition of love, not our own definition. Our definition of love is a wishy-washy, everyone-join-hands-and-sing-kum-ba-ya, hippy-generation inspired kind of "love." This is not true love... it's a lie from hell.

What is the definition of love, according to Scripture?

### 1 John 5:2-3
*By this we know that we love the children of God, when we love God and keep His commandments. For this is the love of God, that we keep His commandments. And His commandments are not burdensome.*

It is impossible to separate the love of God from obeying His commandments, but that is exactly what the mainstream church has attempted to do. The vast majority of our churches preach a love that is *not* defined by Scripture, but defined by our culture, which was heavily influenced by the "flower-power" children of the 60's.

This kind of "love" is straight out of the pit.

Now, in case you think I'm taking you down a rabbit trail, rest assured, I am not. All of this love-talk is directly tied in with false prophets, miracles, signs and wonders. A false prophet will preach a deceptive message, emphasizing a false love spawned by the god of this age.

- This *deceptive* message will devalue holiness, righteousness and the commandments of God, to the point where the listener will be convinced that they might as well throw two-thirds of their Bible away.

- This *deceptive* message equates obedience and zeal for righteousness with "legalism." You will be told that everything was taken care of at the cross, so you don't have to do a thing.

- This *deceptive* message lulls you into spiritual dormancy with attractive, soothing words. **(Isaiah 30:10)**

- This *deceptive* message is often backed up with miracles, signs and wonders and they are ALL performed in the name of Jesus Christ.

But the end result is lawlessness and a cold, cold heart.

When the churchgoer reaches this point, they have a false sense of salvation, and the supernatural signs and wonders will just reinforce their belief. They are absolutely convinced that these signs and wonders come from the Father, and they just might!

To the deceived, signs and wonders are the deciding factor in their analysis of a prophet, but our Messiah showed us the REAL deciding factor in **Matthew 7**. Speaking of false prophets (and many others), Jesus said:

**Matthew 7:21-23**
*Not everyone who says to Me, "Lord, Lord," shall enter*

*the kingdom of heaven, but he who does the will of My Father in heaven. Many will say to Me in that day, "Lord, Lord, have we not prophesied <u>in your name</u>, cast out demons <u>in your name</u>, and done many wonders <u>in your name</u>?" And then I will declare to them, "I never knew you; depart from Me, <u>you who practice lawlessness</u>!"*

When that day comes, it's not going to be whether or not a self-proclaimed prophet performed great heavenly signs and wonders that will determine if he/she makes it into the Kingdom. According to **Matthew 7**, these people apparently "did the stuff" with success! Jesus did not deny the validity of their claims. They actually performed signs and wonders, cast out demons and did many other miracles - <u>all in the name of Jesus</u>!

But apparently, Jesus doesn't care about that.

According to this Scripture, the determining factor for the validity of a person's "ministry" is whether or not they are lawless. It even determines their eternal destination. Think about it.

And if you think this applies ONLY to false prophets, dear reader, think again. Ask yourself - Am I staying true to the commandments of God, or am I sidetracked by the show?

## SUMMING UP THE MAIN POINTS

I understand that this a lot of information regarding miracles, healing, signs and wonders. You're probably thinking, "What am I supposed to do with all this information? What are the take-aways from this commentary?"

Here are the main points in a nutshell.

- *The miraculous is to be a part of the life of the believer, and yet it is used by the enemy (and by God) as a part of the deception of the Last Days.*

- *The miraculous may happen, but it is not what we should pursue. Our responsibility is to obey the Father's commands. HE will decide if (and when) to manifest His power through miracles, signs and wonders.*

- *Craving and seeking signs & wonders is a sign of an <u>"evil and adulterous generation."</u>*

- *Demonic signs and wonders occur when demonic forces are invoked.*

- *It IS possible for God to heal someone in a meeting where His name is being glorified, regardless of who the prophet may be. This has NO BEARING on the validity of the prophet's ministry or the certainty of his/her eternal destination.*

- *Above all, realize that supernatural phenomena are not a "Seal of Approval" from God upon a person's ministry. According to **Matthew 7**, the "Seal of Approval" is given if a person is faithful to keep the commandments of the Most High and teach others to do the same.*

Also, I feel it very important to remind you of something that I discussed earlier in this series.

Remember that a matter is **ESTABLISHED** by 2 or 3 witnesses. Since miracles, signs and wonders can be a gray area for many, it is wise to determine whether or not a prophet is true or false by observing whether any of the other scriptural witnesses are present.

- *Do they perform miracles, signs and wonders and have a huge following?*

- *Do they perform miracles, signs and wonders and lead you away from God's commandments?*

- *Do they perform miracles, signs and wonders and mimic the Holy Spirit?*

If you can see 2 or 3 (or more) distinguishing marks discussed in this book (which were taken right out of the Word of God), then know that this person is indeed a false prophet.

## PRACTICAL ADVICE REGARDING FALSE PROPHETS AND MIRACLES

So let's try to bring this full circle. I want to give some practical advice that, I believe, is firmly backed up by Scripture. We know that the miraculous is to be a part of the life of the believer, and yet it is used by the enemy (and God, as well – **2 Thessalonians 2:9-10**) in the deception of the Last Days.

**First** (and this should be obvious), if someone is performing miracles in their own name or the name of a pagan god, or is using some pagan practice like crystals, voodoo or tarot cards - this isn't God! God does not heal or perform signs and wonders in the name of another god, nor does He use the occult to accomplish His purposes.

Why? Because it glorifies the name of a false god, and not His name.

This should be a "no-brainer," but I thought that I would throw it out there, just in case.

**Second** (and I have to be careful with this one), if someone is performing signs and wonders in the name of Jesus and His name is being glorified, I have no reason to believe that it's the devil doing the work. Why would the enemy want to contribute to God's glorification? Why would He want Jesus' name lifted any higher?

If God can use an ass or a rock **(Luke 19:40)** to glorify His name, He can easily use a false prophet.

**Third**, just because someone may have gotten healed at these revival meetings does not mean that you should attend. In fact, if you know the so-called revivalist is a false prophet, I would highly advise you NOT to go.

God, in His mercy, can (and does) meet people in their ignorance and honors their faith by healing them. If you are NOT ignorant of the enemy's deception and choose to go anyway, what does that say about your faith? Do you really think God will honor it?

**Finally**, if you have received a miracle in the name of Jesus by having hands laid on you, REJOICE! Give God the glory and receive your healing!

Even if that person was found later on to be a false prophet or a huckster, or even questionable… again I say - REJOICE! But don't succumb to the urge to follow whoever it was who laid hands on you. There is no need to collect and absorb all their books, music and teaching.

Don't follow the vessel (they're usually tainted anyway), follow the Messiah, obey His commandments and thank Him for His healing power! Then you will have passed the test!

**Footnotes:**

[1] Blueletter Bible definition of the word "epizēteō" [G1934]
https://www.blueletterbible.org/lang/lexicon/lexicon.cfm?Strongs=G1934&t=N
KJV

.

# SCRIPTURAL WITNESS #9: FALSE PROPHETS PERFORM MIRACLES, SIGNS AND WONDERS (PART 2)

In my 3.5 years of writing, this is probably the most difficult and complex chapter that I've ever had to write - it took me over a month to take it out of the realm of thought and write it down. The delay was frustrating, but I just felt like it was vital that I got this right.

I've never heard anyone talk about this, so this lengthy section is definitely "hot off the press." Grab your Bible, a notebook and a warm cup of coffee and get to a quiet place. This may take a little time for you to get through, but I believe you will find it worth the effort.

## OVERCOMING OUR DENOMINATIONAL CONDITIONING

The topic of "the supernatural" (miracles, signs, wonders, etc.) and its interaction in the life of a believer can be a confusing one. There are various theories, thought processes and numerous "lines in the sand" that exist. And people always seem to camp on the verses that support their particular denominational (or non-denominational) conditioning, to the exclusion of all the other Scriptures that appear to contradict their belief systems.

To those few Bereans who are willing to take an honest look at the Word of God, giving equal value to all the Scripture, this can create many unanswered questions and leave "loose ends" in their theology.

Personally, I absolutely hate to have loose ends in my theology.

Back in the day, when I was young and naive, I would readily embrace every sermon, anecdote and "Word from God" that was passed down from the pastor (or prophet) to the congregation, but now I've put those *"childish ways"* **(1 Corinthians 13:11)** behind me. Now, I need to be convinced that what I am adopting into my belief system is rooted and grounded in the Word of God, not just the latest fad or trendy teaching. If it is a legitimate message, the giver of that message will not feel threatened by any questions posed by the hearer (or reader).

This chapter is an attempt by me to "sew up" a couple of those loose ends that I've had in my theology over the last couple of years in regard to miracles, signs and wonders. I'm not sure that it's completely sewn up yet, but I believe I'm well on my way to finding the answer.

I'm going to present to you my case and ask that you prayerfully consider it. Of course, you don't have to change your theology over it, unless you're absolutely certain that it's confirmed to you by the Holy Spirit and the Word of God. Just chew on it for awhile, file it among the other "possibilities" in your mind, and see if it doesn't influence your thinking a little further down the road.

## SOME TRUTHS STAY TRUE AND INDISPUTABLE... ALWAYS!

The Word of God is indisputable regarding several points. Among them are:

- *God doesn't change* (**Malachi 3:6**);

- *Jesus Christ is the same yesterday, today and forever* (**Hebrews 13:8**);

- *Jesus was the exact representation of the Father* (**Hebrews 1:3**);

- *Jesus spoke the Father's words* (**John 14:10**).

These points must be true at all times, regardless of the circumstances (and regardless of any dispensational understanding), or our faith is in vain. Any doctrine that contradicts these plain and simple truths must be tossed into the trash can with all the other heresies - ALWAYS. If we have any beliefs or mindsets that contradict these plain and simple truths, it is *we* who need to find out why, and *change* our ways of thinking... ALWAYS. It is with this understanding that I ask the following questions, and later on in the chapter, attempt to answer them.

## LOOSE END #1 –
## WHY DOES IT SEEM THAT IT'S ONLY THE FALSE PROPHETS WHO ARE DOING ANY MIRACLES?

Jesus plainly said in His Word that miracles, signs and wonders would follow those who follow Him. The Scriptures could not have been any more clear regarding this point (refer to the prior chapter for supporting Scriptures).

But in this current age of deception, things are not always as they seem. As you look around, it appears that the only people who are doing signs, wonders, healing and miracles are those in the "Word of Faith" and "Prophetic" circles. There are those who would denounce the whole phenomenon and say that it's all a fraud or the work of the devil, but I'm not willing to go that far. In order to support that viewpoint, you have to ignore a lot of evidence and testimony to the contrary.

The truth is, in spite of all the celebrity, fanfare and foolishness, and in spite of all the emotional hype and possible fake healings that occur, there are people who really <u>do</u> get healed in these meetings, and the name of Jesus is lifted up. But it is just as true that these same personalities (in both the "Word of Faith" and "Prophetic" circles) are in gross doctrinal and moral error. That's a problem.

To add to the confusion, I know real, down-to-earth, solid, good-hearted, Bible-following believers who have yet to see anything miraculous at all in their lives. Perhaps you know people like this as well. They are the people who are the warmest, most caring and humble lovers of God that you would ever meet. They would literally give you the shirts off of their backs and yet there doesn't appear to be one iota of the supernatural working in their lives. What's with that???

- *Is God only doling out miracles to the prophetic celebrities?*

- *Are they the only ones worthy to steward the Glory of God?*

- *Are the "good guys" destined to live uneventful lives without miracles?*

- *Are they forever doomed to be perceived as lacking in faith?*

The answer to all of the above questions is **"Of course not!"** Still, these types of questions can make the most relentless Berean want to throw his hands up in the air in frustration and give up. So how do we address this?

Most of you who read my blog[1] do not follow the cessationist line of thinking, which basically believes that the gifts of the Holy Spirit, or any kind of supernatural interaction between God and man, stopped when the apostles died out. If you are like me, you have had too many real supernatural encounters (both good and bad) to give any weight to this thought process.

And the *"God uses imperfect people"* mantra that so many chant nowadays just seems like a weak excuse. At least, it does to me. It's like a "trump card" that people use whenever their favorite prophetic celebrities stumble (for the 100th time), allowing them to keep their prophetic idols where they "belong," permanently enshrined in the altar of the mind.

So again, what do we do with this? How do we reconcile this inconsistency? File these questions in the back of your mind and keep reading.

## LOOSE END #2 –
## IN REGARD TO MIRACLES, SIGNS AND WONDERS
## – DID OUR "UNCHANGEABLE GOD".... CHANGE?

When you study miracles, signs and wonders in the Bible, it appears as if something changes along the way. Jesus told His disciples:

> ### Mark 16:17-18
> *And these signs will follow those who believe: In My name they will cast out demons; they will speak with new tongues; they will take up serpents; and if they drink anything deadly, it will by no means hurt them; they will lay hands on the sick, and they will recover.*

And when someone other than the disciples was casting out demons using His name, our Messiah seemed to have a rather permissive attitude about the situation.

### Mark 9:38-40

*Now John answered Him, saying, "Teacher, we saw someone who does not follow us casting out demons in Your name, and we forbade him because he does not follow us.*

*But Jesus said, "Do not forbid him, for no one who works a miracle in My name can soon afterward speak evil of Me. For he who is not against us is on our side.*

However, after our Savior died and rose again, something happened!

### Acts 19:14-16

*Then some of the itinerant Jewish exorcists took it upon themselves to call the name of the Lord Jesus over those who had evil spirits, saying, "We exorcise you by the Jesus whom Paul preaches."*

*Also there were seven sons of Sceva, a Jewish chief priest, who did so. And the evil spirit answered and said, "Jesus I know, and Paul I know; but who are you?"*

*Then the man in whom the evil spirit was leaped on them, overpowered them, and prevailed against them, so that they fled out of that house naked and wounded.*

None of the above participants were disciples of Jesus, yet one group succeeded and one failed. *Why?* Apparently, what was working for the non-disciple before no longer worked after that pivotal moment when Christ rose again.

Why the apparent change in dynamic?

To add to the confusion, at the End of the Age, we find our risen Messiah rejecting those who do supernatural works in His name, but are not walking according to His Law.

### Matthew 7:21-23

*Not everyone who says to Me, "Lord, Lord," shall enter the kingdom of heaven, but he who does the will of My Father in heaven. Many will say to Me in that day, "Lord, Lord, have we not prophesied <u>in Your name</u>, cast out demons <u>in Your name</u>, and done many wonders <u>in Your name</u>?" And then I will declare to them, "<u>I never knew you; depart from Me, you who practice lawlessness!</u>"*

Again I ask, what happened? *Did our Messiah change His ways?*

No. That can't be possible. If it were possible, then it would contradict the Scripture that says that He never changes! **(Malachi 3:6, Hebrews 1:3, 13:18)**

What do we DO with this? Do we make up our own doctrine to satisfy our questions? Do we just throw it on the back-burner and hope that nobody asks us about this apparent inconsistency in Scripture? Or do we take up the ridiculous answer of some false prophets who say, *"God never changes…. except when He does?"*

No! We take up the honor of kings, and we search it out! Come on, people, studying the Bible is fun!

I'm going to assure you right off the bat that everything is alright; our Messiah did not change. The Word of God is always true and consistent. So how do we reconcile these questions that are out there? I think I might have an answer.

## UNDERSTANDING MIRACLES, SIGNS AND WONDERS WITHIN THE CONTEXT OF TWO WARRING KINGDOMS

In order to properly understand miracles, signs and wonders and their role in the life of a believer, it greatly helps to think of it within the context of what I call "the Kingdom Invasion Process." Does that sound too far out in left field? Just stick with me, I think you'll get it before the end of this chapter.

We, as believers, understand that there are two kingdoms: the Kingdom of Light and the kingdom of darkness. Right now, we find ourselves in the middle of a kingdom invasion. Our Messiah's Kingdom (the Kingdom of Light) is in the process of invading the kingdom of darkness (Lucifer's kingdom – the world). All of the spiritual powers and inhabitants of this world are going to be either annihilated or assimilated into His Kingdom.

But this invasion is not yet complete. We have to wait for the End of the Age for this to occur, when the seventh angel will announce:

### Revelation 11:15b
*The kingdoms of this world have become the kingdoms of our Lord and of His Christ, and He shall reign forever and ever!*

We have not yet heard the seventh angel sound. Heaven has not yet declared this invasion is over because the spiritual and physical *"kingdoms of this world"* are not fully conquered.

Think about this, you who abuse the idea of the *"finished work of Christ."* The *"It is finished"* **(John 19:30)** uttered at the cross is not the same as the *"It is done"* **(Revelation 21:6)** that will be spoken at the End of the Age.

## THE KINGDOM INVASION BEGINS

Prior to the Messiah's birth, the prophets prophesied of this Kingdom invasion. Then, when John the Baptist began his ministry, the Kingdom of Heaven's advance on the kingdoms of this world commenced. Jesus said:

### Matthew 11:12-13

*And from the days of John the Baptist until now the kingdom of heaven suffers violence [has been steadily advancing - NLT], and the violent take it by force. For all the prophets and the law prophesied until John.*

From the time John was cast into prison, Jesus started to preach *"Repent: for the kingdom of heaven is at hand."*

### Matthew 4:17 (Read verse 12-17 for full context)

*From that time Jesus began to preach, and to say, Repent: for the kingdom of heaven is at hand.*

He told His disciples to preach this same message (paraphrased): *"Repent! Change your ways, for the Kingdom of Heaven is advancing on this kingdom! Forsake your ways and learn God's Ways… for this world's system is about to come under the authority of another Kingdom!"*

And to prove that what they said was true, they were to perform miracles, signs and wonders.

### Matthew 10:7-8

*And as ye go, preach, saying, "The kingdom of heaven is at hand." Heal the sick, cleanse the lepers, raise the dead, cast out devils: freely ye have received, freely give.*

Scripture makes it abundantly clear that miracles, signs and wonders are the demonstration of God's power.

**Psalm 66:3**

*Say to God, "How awesome are Your works! Through the greatness of Your power Your enemies shall submit themselves to You."*

**Exodus 7:3**

*And I will harden Pharaoh's heart, and multiply My signs and My wonders in the land of Egypt.*

**Deuteronomy 4:34**

*Or did God ever try to go and take for Himself a nation from the midst of another nation, by trials, by signs, by wonders, by war, by a mighty hand and an outstretched arm, and by great terrors, according to all that the LORD your God did for you in Egypt before your eyes?*

**Deuteronomy 6:20-22**

*When your son asks you in time to come, saying, 'What is the meaning of the testimonies, the statutes, and the judgments which the LORD our God has commanded you?' then you shall say to your son: 'We were slaves of Pharaoh in Egypt, and the LORD brought us out of Egypt with a mighty hand; and the LORD showed signs and wonders before our eyes, great and severe, against Egypt, Pharaoh, and all his household.*

When Jesus walked the earth and the Kingdom of Light began to infiltrate the kingdom of darkness, things started changing in this world. Supernatural activity (the demonstration of God's Power) was being felt in the land of Israel.

## PARABLES OF THE INVADING KINGDOM

When Jesus taught His disciples about the Kingdom of Heaven, He described the Kingdom as something that starts out really small, but then turns into something massive!

## Matthew 13:31-33

*Another parable He put forth to them, saying: "The kingdom of heaven is like a mustard seed, which a man took and sowed in his field, which indeed is the least of all the seeds; but when it is grown it is greater than the herbs and becomes a tree, so that the birds of the air come and nest in its branches."*

*Another parable He spoke to them: "The kingdom of heaven is like leaven, which a woman took and hid in three measures of meal till it was all leavened."*

Generally speaking, this is what it's like when an army invades. At first, it can affect only one area, usually around the surrounding wall, or border, of a nation, but after awhile, it affects every area of life. Eventually, the whole nation knows that it's being invaded and it gets very personal.

2000 years ago, this is what the invasion of the Kingdom of Light would have been like. Sure, in Jerusalem and the immediate surrounding area, the commencement of this invasion by the forces of Light was well-known. Jesus' ministry was making very large ripples! But to the surrounding, distant nations (meaning Europe, Africa, and the Orient), the Good News had yet to be preached. They had no clue that their world was being invaded by another army.

## THE IMPACT OF THE KINGDOM INVASION

Although the invasion would start out small, it would pack a powerful punch!

Now, think about this for a minute. If you were the commander of an army and wanted to invade another kingdom, what would be the best strategy?

If I were in charge of the invading Army, I would think that it would be in the best interest of my forces to knock out the "big guns" of the enemy first. Completely humiliate the enemy and wipe out any remaining weaponry that could be used against my army as it invades the territory that I desire to conquer.

This is what Jesus accomplished by His ministry, death and resurrection - and He used the miraculous to do it.

### Matthew 28:18
*And Jesus came and spoke to them, saying, "All authority has been given to Me in heaven and on earth."*

### Colossians 2:15
*Having disarmed principalities and powers, He made a public spectacle of them, triumphing over them in it.*

### Revelation 1:18
*I am He who lives, and was dead, and behold, I am alive forevermore. Amen. And I have the keys of Hades and of Death.*

### 1 John 3:8
*He who sins is of the devil, for the devil has sinned from the beginning. For this purpose the Son of God was manifested, that He might destroy the works of the devil.*

Take another look at that last verse. Notice that it did not say that the Messiah was manifested to destroy *the devil?* Yeshua was manifested to destroy <u>THE WORKS</u> of the devil! This means that everything the devil set up as part of his kingdom - all of his "big guns" - were destroyed by the death and resurrection of the Messiah.

The devil gets his due at a later date. That's when the party starts!

## SENDING IN THE GROUND FORCES

As the invasion continues, however, the strategy of the Kingdom changes with it. The "big guns" of the enemy are demolished, and now the ground forces can go in and conquer the territory for the invading Kingdom.

**PLEASE NOTE:** This is NOT reflective of a change in the Father; He is always the same and His ways are always the same (and it's the same with the Son). But now the enemy is on the run! Satan has been stripped of his primary means of defense, and the troops are on his heels!

Jesus spoke of this in what is known as the "Olivet Discourse." Before you read the remainder of this chapter, I highly recommend that you read all of **Matthew 24 and 25** for context and assistance in your understanding.

After speaking in **Matthew 24** about the end time events that were to occur before His return (including a warning to beware of false prophets that perform false signs and wonders – v24), Jesus says something really interesting:

> **Matthew 24:42-25:1a**
> *Watch therefore, for you do not know what hour your Lord is coming.*
>
> *But know this, that if the master of the house had known what hour the thief would come, he would have watched and not allowed his house to be broken into. Therefore you also be ready, for the Son of Man is coming at an hour you do not expect.*
>
> *Who then is a faithful and wise servant, whom his master made ruler over his household, to give them food in due season? Blessed is that servant whom his master, when he comes, will find so doing. Assuredly, I say to you that he will make him ruler over all his goods.*

*But if that evil servant says in his heart, "My master is delaying his coming," and begins to beat his fellow servants, and to eat and drink with the drunkards, the master of that servant will come on a day when he is not looking for him and at an hour that he is not aware of, and will cut him in two and appoint him his portion with the hypocrites. There shall be weeping and gnashing of teeth.*

*THEN the kingdom of heaven shall be likened to ten virgins ...*

I realize that I combined the beginning and ending of two chapters here. Keep in mind, Jesus never spoke in chapter and verse; all of these divisions were put into the Bible by man. If you can remember that, it will revolutionize your study of the Word.

We see here a change in the dynamic of the way the Kingdom operates with mankind. And since the Kingdom goes hand-in-hand with miracles, signs and wonders, I see no reason to "un-link" them here.

When this invasion started, it was all about INCREASE. The Kingdom Invasion started small, and grew larger and larger really fast! That's why Jesus was fine with the non-disciple casting out demons, even though he wasn't following Him.

Now that most of the work is accomplished, now that the "big guns" are demolished, the Kingdom becomes all about REDUCTION. That's right! I said it! The Word of Faith people are completely wrong! In this Age, the Kingdom is going to decrease... not in scope... not in authority... but in membership!

Does that sound blasphemous? Please keep in mind that *"the Way is narrow,"* and keep reading.

## REDUCTION IN THE KINGDOM

Notice the way in which Jesus talks about all of these signs and events that would happen, signaling the End of the Age. If you study your Bible and history, you would know that the "signs" spoken of in **Matthew 24** started occurring right after Yeshua died and rose again. Persecution, famines, crazy people doing signs and wonders... they are all there in the book of Acts, and they have been happening ever since!

Jesus talks to His disciples about the importance of watching, cautioning them about being evil servants and revealing to them the penalty - then He says something interesting.

He says: *"THEN the Kingdom of Heaven shall be like..."*

This signifies a change in the Kingdom dynamic. The Kingdom operated one way up to a certain point, and then it operated another way after that point. Read all of **Matthew 25** and contemplate the following points.

- The ten virgins were **all virgins** and they were **all waiting** for the Bridegroom to come; they were not pagans and sinners. Yet their number was <u>reduced</u> from ten to five. **Why?** - *No oil of consecration*

- In the next parable, God invested in **His servants**. They were **all servants of God**, not sinners, but one of the three was *"cast into outer darkness"* where there is *"weeping and gnashing of teeth."* **Why?** - *Because he was wicked, lazy and unprofitable* **(Matthew 25:26, 30)**.

- When God gathers the nations before Him, He judges between the sheep and the goats. What is the deciding factor? Contrary to popular belief, it's not the altruistic acts of feeding and clothing the poor, visiting people in prison, etc. – although those are important things to do.

The Messiah says in **verse 40** *"inasmuch as you did it to one of the least of these My brethren."*

**Who are the Messiah's "brethren?"**

### Matthew 12:48-50
*But He answered and said to the one who told Him, "Who is My mother and who are My brothers?" And He stretched out His hand toward His disciples and said, "Here are My mother and My brothers! <u>For whoever does the will of My Father in heaven is My brother and sister and mother.</u>"*

**What is the "Will of God?"**

### 1 Thessalonians 4:3-8
<u>*For this is the will of God, your sanctification:*</u> *that you should abstain from sexual immorality; that each of you should know how to possess his own vessel in sanctification and honor, not in passion of lust, like the Gentiles who do not know God; that no one should take advantage of and defraud his brother in this matter, because the Lord is the avenger of all such, as we also forewarned you and testified.*

*For God did not call us to uncleanness, but in holiness. Therefore he who rejects this does not reject man, but God, who has also given us His Holy Spirit.*

### 1 John 2:15-17
*Do not love the world or the things in the world. If anyone loves the world, the love of the Father is not in him. For all that is in the world – the lust of the flesh, the lust of the eyes, and the pride of life – is not of the Father but is of the world. And the world is passing*

*away, and the lust of it; <u>but he who does the will of God abides forever</u>.*

So we can see the following factors coming into play, pertaining to whether you are "In" or "Out" of the Kingdom:

- **Having the Oil of Consecration** – being consecrated to His purposes, obeying His Word (which is His will)

- **Being faithful with what He has given you** – not being wicked (twisted), lazy and unprofitable

- **Giving of your time and substance** to those doing the will of God – His brethren

**WHOAH!** Whatever happened to **Mark 9:40** *"For he who is not against us is on our side?"*

So much for an easy and carefree entry into the Kingdom, right? The Way is definitely narrow, and few there be that find it. This could be a H-U-G-E study, but it's outside the scope of this book. I really want to stick with the theme of "signs and wonders" here.

We can see that, after Jesus died and rose again, it was no longer acceptable to perform signs and wonders without being disciples of the Messiah. Just ask the sons of Sceva! Furthermore, at the End of the Age, we will see EVEN MORE of a decrease, as those who performed all kinds of wonderful miracles, signs and wonders IN JESUS NAME are turned away due to their lawlessness.

### Matthew 7:21-23
*Not everyone who says to Me, "Lord, Lord," shall enter the kingdom of heaven, but he who does the will of My Father in heaven. Many will say to Me in that day, "Lord, Lord, have we not prophesied in Your name, cast out demons in Your name, and done many wonders in*

*Your name?" And then I will declare to them, "I never knew you; depart from Me, you who practice lawlessness!"* [2][3]

## ANSWERING THE QUESTIONS

Understanding the role of miracles, signs and wonders within the context of a Kingdom Invasion puts us in a better "frame-of-mind" to answer the two questions posed at the beginning of this lengthy chapter.

Let's look at them again. Let me start with Loose End #2.

**Loose End #2 – In regard to miracles, signs and wonders – did our "Unchangeable God" ...change?**

The obvious answer to this question is "No." He is the same miracle-working God that He was during the Exodus from Egypt and during the Messiah's first appearance. We simply cannot arrive at the conclusion that God changed somehow, if the Scripture says He never changes.

Let's get this firmly ingrained into our theology: our God never changes. He is the same God in the Old Testament, in the New Testament and "all the parts in between" and after.

At the risk of sounding repetitive, He didn't change - but as this Kingdom Invasion progressed, with the "big guns" of the enemy completely destroyed, He can and does use other methods to establish His rule. Miracles, signs and wonders are still part of His "arsenal," but there is something that changed in the Kingdom dynamic after the Messiah died and rose again. I will attempt to describe it in Loose End #1.

**Loose End #1 – Why does it seem that it's only the false prophets who are doing any miracles?**

This may be a little tough to swallow, but there is something that you need to understand before we go on. Here it goes:

*The reason God heals and performs signs, wonders and miracles is NOT to make you feel better or impress you!*

The reason God performs miracles, signs, wonders and healing is to *confirm His Word*.

## MIRACLES, SIGNS AND WONDERS CONFIRM THE WORD OF GOD

Miracles, signs and wonders were performed to *confirm His word* spoken to Moses and Aaron.

### Exodus 4:30-31
*And Aaron spake all the words which the LORD had spoken unto Moses, and did the signs in the sight of the people. And the people believed: and when they heard that the LORD had visited the children of Israel, and that he had looked upon their affliction, then they bowed their heads and worshiped.*

Miracles, signs and wonders were performed by Jesus to *confirm His word that* He spoke. Indeed, He was THE Word, so He was confirming Himself!

### John 2:23
*Now when he was in Jerusalem at the passover, in the feast day, many believed in his name, when they saw the miracles which he did.*

### John 3:2
*This man [Nicodemus] came to Jesus by night and said*

*to Him, "Rabbi, we know that You are a teacher come from God; for no one can do these signs that You do unless God is with him."*

Miracles, signs and wonders were performed to *confirm God's word*, preached by His disciples.

### Mark 16:20
*And they went forth, and preached everywhere, the Lord working with them, and confirming the word with signs following. Amen.*

### Acts 8:5-6
*Then Philip went down to the city of Samaria, and preached Christ unto them. And the people with one accord gave heed unto those things which Philip spake, hearing and seeing the miracles which he did.*

Do you see a pattern here? It's all about *confirming God's Word*. Feeling better or being impressed with the works of God is just a wonderful side benefit.

So, why are the hucksters doing miracles? Is God confirming the word spoken by false prophets?

In short... yes.

Let us take a look at **Mark 16** again:

### Mark 16:20
And they went forth, and preached everywhere, the Lord working with *them*, and confirming the word with signs following. Amen.

Notice the word "them" is italicized? This means that the translators (who were mortal, fallible men) inserted the word in the text. They did this to help clarify things the best they knew how, but in this case (and in many other Scriptures), it had the opposite effect. Let's re-look at the Scripture, omitting the text that was not supposed to be there in the first place.

**Mark 16:20**
*And they went forth, and preached everywhere, <u>the Lord working with and confirming the word</u> with signs following. Amen.*

God was working with and confirming His word - not the disciples.

And (surprise, surprise) God is the same today. He works with and confirms His word, not man. Regardless of the circumstances - regardless of the way that it is preached, it is the Word that gets confirmed by miracles, signs and wonders. Yes, the Word of God is <u>that powerful</u>.

**Hebrews 4:12-13**
*For the word of God is living and powerful, and sharper than any two-edged sword, piercing even to the division of soul and spirit, and of joints and marrow, and is a discerner of the thoughts and intents of the heart.*

*And there is no creature hidden from His sight, but all things are naked and open to the eyes of Him to whom we must give account.*

So this point answers our questions:

- *Why did the Jewish itinerant exorcists and seven sons of Sceva fail?*

- *Why did the non-disciple during Jesus' time on earth apparently succeed?*

- *Why does it seem that it is the false prophets who are doing miracles?*

The seven sons of Sceva **(Acts 19:14-16)** FAILED to cast out the demon because they were trusting in the Name of Jesus without preaching or identifying with the Word of God (at least, there is no evidence of it). In their arrogance, they attempted to overcome a supernatural being by proclaiming *"We exorcise you by the Jesus whom Paul preaches."* The demon was empowered to beat them senseless because there was nothing in the seven sons of Sceva to withstand the evil.

The non-disciple who SUCCEEDED in casting out a demon **(Mark 9:38-40)** while Jesus was on the earth did so because, as I've stated before, miracles, signs and wonders are used to *confirm the Word*! So it is a logical assumption that the Word must have been preached in some way.

God uses miracles, signs and wonders where the Word is preached, to confirm that Word, regardless of the way it is preached. Say what you will about the "Word of Faith" and the "Prophetic Movement" (and I have a lot to say), but I have to concede that they will quote Bible verses and elaborate/preach on them (for better or worse).

## A FINAL INVITATION

Why would God choose to operate this way? I believe that it is due to His mercy.

I believe that the healings, miracles, signs and wonders that occur in Jesus' name among the false prophets are a last ditch effort by God to confirm His Word in those who have rejected it. It is an act of mercy to extend a final invitation to those who have not yet confirmed the Word in themselves, and it is an act of kindness to those who have.

The Kingdom Invasion is almost complete, and those who will not bow to the supremacy of the laws of His Kingdom will find themselves in a precarious position.

## Matthew 7:21-23

*Not everyone who says to Me, "Lord, Lord," shall enter the kingdom of heaven, but he who does the will of My Father in heaven. Many will say to Me in that day, "Lord, Lord, have we not prophesied in Your name, cast out demons in Your name, and done many wonders in Your name?" And then I will declare to them, "I never knew you; depart from Me, you who practice lawlessness!"*

People, you DON'T want to be in the camp of the lawless when He returns. It doesn't matter if you have performed miracles or received miracles. If you don't submit to the rule of the invading Kingdom, you are going to hear *"depart from me,"* and it's going to be a bitter day for you. The thoughts and intents of your heart will be laid bare, and everyone will know what He knew all along - that His Word found no place in your heart.

## John 15:10

*If ye keep my commandments, ye shall abide in my love; even as I have kept my Father's commandments, and abide in his love.*

**Footnote:**

[1] Web site: http://www.honorofkings.org

[2] Blueletter bible definition of the word "anomia" [G458]

https://www.blueletterbible.org/lang/lexicon/lexicon.cfm?Strongs=G458&t=KJV

[3] Blueletter bible definition of the word "anomos" [G459]

https://www.blueletterbible.org/lang/lexicon/lexicon.cfm?strongs=G459&t=KJV

# SCRIPTURAL WITNESS #10: FALSE PROPHETS PRODUCE BAD FRUIT (PART 1)

For this last scriptural witness, I would like to dig deeper into a characteristic that I introduced in a blog post I wrote a couple of years ago entitled *"False Prophets, Fruit and the Unwitting Wolf."* I've included it in **Appendix B** for you, as supplemental information.

Producing bad fruit may seem like a cut-and-dried concept to grasp. One does not need to look very far to see the sexual immorality, error and greed that are rampant in the "Word of Faith" and "Prophetic" movements. But there is a lot more to the concept of "bad fruit" than meets the eye.

The core verse of this chapter (and the next) is going to be **Matthew 7:15-16**.

> **Matthew 7:15-16**
> *Beware of false prophets, who come to you in sheep's clothing, but inwardly they are ravenous wolves. You will know them by their fruits.* <u>**Do men gather grapes from thorn bushes or figs from thistles?**</u>

Most students of the Bible will gloss over this passage and assume that Jesus was only teaching on false prophets, and that you cannot get something *good* out of something *bad*. This is not an incorrect way of looking at this verse, but it is definitely an *incomplete* way.

If you had been an Israelite during the days that Jesus walked the earth, you would have had a much greater understanding of what our Master was teaching. You see, to the first century Jew, grapes, thorns, figs and thistles were much more significant.

## ISRAEL'S PROMISE – THE IMPORTANCE OF GRAPES AND FIGS

Unlike the modern day church, the nation of Israel heard the writings of the Prophets read in the synagogues every Sabbath. Because of this, they were very familiar with the concept and purpose of the grape and the fig. They knew that grapes and figs were some of the first fruits taken from the Promised Land when Israel first came to its border.

> **Numbers 13:23**
> *Then they came to the Valley of Eshcol, <u>and there cut down a branch with one cluster of grapes</u>; they carried it between two of them on a pole. They also brought some of the pomegranates <u>and figs</u>.*

In the writings of the Prophets (and elsewhere in Scripture), there is a close association between the condition of the fig tree, the strength of the vine, and Israel's relationship with God. When God blessed the land of Israel, His children would dwell securely *"each man under his vine and his fig tree."*

> **1 Kings 4:24-25**
> *For he had dominion over all the region on this side of the River from Tiphsah even to Gaza, namely over all the kings on this side of the River; and he had peace on every side all around him. And Judah and Israel dwelt safely, <u>each man under his vine and his fig tree</u>, from Dan as far as Beersheba, all the days of Solomon.*

When they walked in disobedience to His commands and were punished, the vines and the fig trees were always affected adversely.

### Jeremiah 8:12-13
*Were they ashamed when they had committed abomination?*
*No! They were not at all ashamed,*
*Nor did they know how to blush.*
*Therefore they shall fall among those who fall;*
*In the time of their punishment*
*They shall be cast down," says the LORD.*

*"I will surely consume them," says the LORD.*
*"No grapes shall be on the vine,*
*Nor figs on the fig tree,*
*And the leaf shall fade;*
*And the things I have given them shall pass away from them."*

### Hosea 2:12
*And I will destroy her vines and her fig trees, Of which she has said, "These are my wages that my lovers have given me." So I will make them a forest, and the beasts of the field shall eat them.*

### Joel 1:7
*He has laid waste My vine, and ruined My fig tree;*
*He has stripped it bare and thrown it away; its branches are made white.*

When Jesus walked the earth (the first time), the children of Israel were looking for a day when their Messiah would come and release them from Roman bondage. They were all well aware of what the Prophets said about this Kingdom.

### Micah 4:1-4

*But in the last days it shall come to pass, that the mountain of the house of the LORD shall be established in the top of the mountains, and it shall be exalted above the hills; and people shall flow unto it.*

*And many nations shall come, and say, Come, and let us go up to the mountain of the LORD, and to the house of the God of Jacob; and he will teach us of his ways, and we will walk in his paths: for the law shall go forth of Zion, and the word of the LORD from Jerusalem.*

*And he shall judge among many people, and rebuke strong nations afar off; and they shall beat their swords into plowshares, and their spears into pruninghooks: nation shall not lift up a sword against nation, neither shall they learn war any more.*

*But they shall sit every man under his vine and under his fig tree; and none shall make them afraid: for the mouth of the LORD of hosts hath spoken it.*

### Zechariah 3:8-10

*"Hear, O Joshua, the high priest,*
*You and your companions who sit before you,*
*For they are a wondrous sign;*
*For behold, I am bringing forth My Servant the BRANCH.*

*For behold, the stone*
*That I have laid before Joshua:*
*Upon the stone are seven eyes.*
*Behold, I will engrave its inscription,"*
*Says the LORD of hosts,*
*"And I will remove the iniquity of that land in one day."*

> *"In that day," says the LORD of hosts, "Everyone will invite his neighbor under his vine and under his fig tree."*

So when Jesus spoke of grapes and figs, it caused His listeners to take notice! They knew what the message of a true prophet would sound like. Like I said earlier, every Sabbath they would hear readings from the Prophets in the synagogue! Jesus likened the fruit of the message and ministry of a true prophet to grapes and figs. Conversely, He likened the fruit of the message and ministry of a false prophet to thorns and thistles.

Are you making a connection here? Good!

In this chapter (and the next), we're going to study these different types of fruit and what they symbolized. I understand that determining symbolism can be somewhat subjective in nature, but the Word is pretty specific about grapes, figs, thorns and thistles. I'm confident that, when you're done reading these two chapters, you'll have a better grasp of what Jesus was inferring and a clearer picture of the false prophet.

## GRAPES = VESSELS OF RESTORATION/BLESSING

Restoration, which will be fully realized at the End of the Age, is the whole point of our salvation "walk" with God. We want to be restored back to the original, sinless state that Adam dwelt in when he walked with God in the Garden of Eden. We want to see our Father face-to-face and to speak with Him without this dimensional veil between us.

If you go by the "law of first mentions,"[1] grapes are closely associated with this concept of restoration. The first time we see the word "grapes" being used is in **Genesis 40**.

### Genesis 40:9-13, 21

*Then the chief butler told his dream to Joseph, and said to him,"Behold, in my dream a vine was before me, and in the vine were three branches; it was as though it budded, its blossoms shot forth, **and its clusters brought forth ripe grapes**. Then Pharaoh's cup was in my hand; and I took the grapes and pressed them into Pharaoh's cup, and placed the cup in Pharaoh's hand."*

*And Joseph said to him, "This is the interpretation of it: The three branches are three days. Now within three days Pharaoh will lift up your head and **restore** you to your place, and you will put Pharaoh's cup in his hand according to the former manner, when you were his butler."*

*...Then he **restored** the chief butler to his butlership again, and he placed the cup in Pharaoh's hand."*

We see here in the chief butler's dream that, once the grapes are ripe, he is restored to his original position.

Israel knew that grapes (and figs) symbolized their nation at the first, when they were taken out of Egypt and wandered in the wilderness.

### Hosea 9:10

*I found Israel like grapes in the wilderness; I saw your fathers as the first ripe in the fig tree at her first time: but they went to Baal Peor, and separated themselves unto that shame; and their abominations were according as they loved.*

### Jeremiah 2:2-3

*Go and cry in the hearing of Jerusalem, saying, "Thus says the LORD:*

*'I remember you,*
*The kindness of your youth,*
*The love of your betrothal,*
*When you went after Me in the wilderness,*
*In a land not sown.*

*Israel was holiness to the LORD,*
*The firstfruits of His increase.*
*All that devour him will offend;*
*Disaster will come upon them,' says the LORD."*

God intended Israel to be His priests, representatives and ambassadors to the world to show them the Way to serve the Father. This would fulfill His word to Abraham.

### Genesis 22:17-18
*...blessing I will bless you, and multiplying I will multiply your descendants as the stars of the heaven and as the sand which is on the seashore; and your descendants shall possess the gate of their enemies. In your seed all the nations of the earth shall be blessed, because you have obeyed My voice.*

### Exodus 19:5-6
*"Now therefore, if you will indeed obey My voice and keep My covenant, then you shall be a special treasure to Me above all people; for all the earth is Mine. And you shall be to Me a kingdom of priests and a holy nation." These are the words which you shall speak to the children of Israel.*

### Deuteronomy 4:5-8 (NLT)
*Look, I now teach you these decrees and regulations just as the LORD my God commanded me, so that you may obey them in the land you are about to enter and occupy.*

*Obey them completely, and you will display your wisdom and intelligence among the surrounding nations. When they hear all these decrees, they will exclaim, "How wise and prudent are the people of this great nation!"*

*For what great nation has a god as near to them as the LORD our God is near to us whenever we call on him? And what great nation has decrees and regulations as righteous and fair as this body of instructions that I am giving you today?*

God wanted the nation of Israel to be His "go-between" and assist Him in the restoration of planet Earth. Whoever would choose to change their ways and follow His ways would embark upon the path of restoration.

Isaiah said that grapes are containers of blessing.

### Isaiah 65:8
*Thus says the LORD: "As the new wine is found in the cluster, and one says, 'Do not destroy it, <u>for a blessing is in it</u>,' so will I do for My servants' sake, that I may not destroy them all."*

So it's only logical to draw the conclusion that, if Israelites were the grapes, then they were to be *"containers of blessing"* for the people of the earth. How would the blessing of God come to the people of the earth? When they repented and obeyed His Word!

You see, when an Israelite sought for grapes from an alleged prophet, he/she sought for fruit that would bless them (the seeker) and assist in their restoration as the people of God.

**For further study:** Where do grapes come from?

**Answer:** A vine! In the Old Testament, vines always represented nations. Israel was a nation who was portrayed as a vine **(Hosea 10:1, Joel 1:7, Jeremiah 2:20-21)** and so was Sodom **(Deuteronomy 32:32)**.

**More study:** What was the "blessing" that Israel contained? It was the wine and the "new wine!"

## FIGS = REPENTANCE, FREEDOM FROM SIN

When we read about figs in the Word of God, we find that they are closely associated with repentance and freedom from sin. When Adam and Eve sinned in the Garden of Eden, they sewed fig leaves together to cover their nakedness.

> **Genesis 3:7**
> *Then the eyes of both of them were opened, and they knew that they were naked; <u>and they sewed fig leaves together and made themselves coverings</u>.*

Before we go on, notice that it wasn't the *fruits* of the fig tree that covered their nakedness, but the *leaves*. There is a difference between having your sin covered and actually being rid of your sin. So, the LEAVES of the fig tree symbolize a covering for sin.

The FRUIT of the fig tree, however, symbolizes repentance. How do we know this?

We read in **2 Kings 20** that King Hezekiah was on the verge of death due to a boil, but because the king tearfully repented, God told the prophet Isaiah to have the King put a *"lump of figs"* on the boil, and it was healed.

> **2 Kings 20:7**
> *Then Isaiah said, "Take a lump of figs." So they took and laid it on the boil, and he recovered.*

After Jesus spoke to His disciples of repentance in **Luke 13:1-5**, He told a parable of a fig tree.

> **Luke 13:6-9**
> *He also spoke this parable: "A certain man had a fig tree planted in his vineyard, and he came seeking fruit on it and found none. Then he said to the keeper of his vineyard, "<u>Look, for three years I have come seeking fruit on this fig tree and find none</u>. Cut it down; why does it use up the ground?"*
>
> *But he answered and said to him, "Sir, let it alone this year also, until I dig around it and fertilize it. And if it bears fruit, well. But if not, after that you can cut it down."*

We see in Mark that Jesus cursed the fig tree because He saw leaves on the tree (symbolic of the nation of Israel), but no fruit.

> **Mark 11:13**
> *And seeing from afar a fig tree having leaves, He went to see if perhaps He would find something on it. When He came to it, He found nothing but leaves, for it was not the season for figs.*

Jesus saw the artificial covering for sin, but no actual repentance.

**For further study:** Where do figs come from?

**Answer:** a fig tree! **(Hosea 9:10, Joel 1:7)**

## THE MINISTRY OF THE GRAPE/FIG

So, from the Scriptures provided, we can see that the nation of Israel is compared to many types of plant life:

- both the vine and the grapes ON the vine;

- both the fig tree and the figs ON the tree.

There is a reason for this.

The nation of Israel was to be a vessel of blessing and restoration to the world around them. They were to provide an example of what it meant to repent from earthly ways and take on the ways of the Most High. Not only that, they were to *produce* more vessels of blessing and restoration, who have repented and followed the Great King.

In other words, they were to be His prophets.

### 1 Chronicles 16:16-22

*The covenant which He made with Abraham, and His oath to Isaac, and confirmed it to Jacob for a statute, to Israel for an everlasting covenant, saying, "To you I will give the land of Canaan as the allotment of your inheritance," When you were few in number, indeed very few, and strangers in it.*

*When they went from one nation to another, and from one kingdom to another people, He permitted no man to do them wrong; Yes, He rebuked kings for their sakes, saying, "Do not touch My anointed ones, and do My prophets no harm."* **(Also see also Psalm 105:9-15.)**

## TYING IT ALL TOGETHER

Let's come back to Jesus and the Sermon on the Mount, specifically **Matthew 7**.

Speaking of false prophets, Jesus said that it was impossible to get grapes and figs from thorns and thistles (thornbushes).

The "fig" (repentance) and the "grape" (restoration/blessing) were the fruits of ALL the prophets up until that point in time when Jesus walked the earth. Jesus was affirming the use of this same criteria for the discernment of all future prophets.

Notice that the Messiah did **not** say, *"There are going to be prophets after me who are only going to say nice things to you! And, if they do signs and wonders in my name, that's who you need to follow! They are my chosen!"*

Right after giving this "fruit comparison," the Master says:

> **Matthew 7:20-23**
> *Therefore by their fruits you will know them.*
>
> *Not everyone who says to Me, "Lord, Lord," shall enter the kingdom of heaven, but he who does the will of My Father in heaven.*
>
> *Many will say to Me in that day, "Lord, Lord, have we not prophesied in Your name, cast out demons in Your name, and done many wonders in Your name?"*
>
> *And then I will declare to them, "I never knew you; depart from Me, you who practice lawlessness!"*

In the next chapter, we will discuss thorns and thistles, the fruit of the false prophets.

**Footnotes:**

[1] See http://thelawoffirstmention.com/

# SCRIPTURAL WITNESS #10: FALSE PROPHETS PRODUCE BAD FRUIT (PART 2)

In the last chapter, we discussed the fruit of a true prophet, which would be restoration and blessing (grapes) as well as repentance and evidence of righteousness (figs). This is the "fruit" that should nourish those who seek out the ministry of a prophet. Now we're going to discuss the bad fruit that people receive when they interact with a false prophet. This goes way beyond the "surface-level" idolatry, sexual immorality and greed that you see in today's charismatic circles.

Like the grapes and figs, thorns and thistles have a much deeper meaning.

## THORNS & THISTLES WORK TOGETHER

Unlike the grape and the fig, thorns and thistles are a little more difficult to assign individual symbolism to. After all, they are almost the same in their characteristics and appearance. Rather, we see in the Scripture that they work together as a team to accomplish the same purpose - to choke the Word planted in your heart.

Answersingenesis.org really hits the nail on the head with this commentary on thorns and thistles:

> *Many thorny plants, nettles, brambles and thistles are considered to be weeds. These are usually the first invaders of broken-up or abandoned (fallow) soil. We*

*know the reason for this is because many of these plants are the product of cursed ground (Genesis 3). Weeds have the ability to grow in harsh conditions and have abundant seeds with well-engineered dispersal mechanisms for populating open areas. Weeds will steal the essential nutrients from the soil the intended crop requires. By definition, weeds overgrow or choke out more desirable plants.*[1]

This is a very rich chunk of text with several points worthy of their own study, but time and space prevent me from commenting on each one. The first thing that stood out to me is that thorns and thistles are a product of cursed ground. This is backed up by the Word of God.

### Genesis 3:17-18

*Then to Adam He said, "Because you have heeded the voice of your wife, and have eaten from the tree of which I commanded you, saying, 'You shall not eat of it': "Cursed is the ground for your sake; in toil you shall eat of it all the days of your life. Both thorns and thistles it shall bring forth for you, and you shall eat the herb of the field."*

This is a vital point to understand about the words and ministry of a false prophet.

Many people write to me, saying *"Prophet so-and-so may have started out with his/her heart in the right place, but then they were lured away because of the money/fame/etc."* As much as I wish that were true, I have to disagree. You see, soil will produce fruit from whatever seeds are planted in it - all you have to do is add a little water.

### Matthew 7:17-18

*Even so, every good tree bears good fruit, but a bad tree*

*bears bad fruit. A good tree cannot bear bad fruit, nor can a bad tree bear good fruit.*

If we take this analogy further, it would be only logical to assume that a bad tree comes from a bad seed and a good tree comes from a good seed, or "like-begets-like."

Of course, there is always room for repentance, where you can allow God to destroy the bad tree and uproot the evil seed, but unfortunately, this is the exception rather than the norm. Nobody wants to face (or admit) that their entire ministry is based on lies and deception.

That would definitely be a bitter pill to swallow.

Let's go back to thorns and thistles.

## THISTLES DAMAGE THE GROWTH OF THE WORD

Other than its destructive partnership with thorns, the Word doesn't have a lot to say about thistles. The word "thistle" comes from the Greek word **"tribolos" [G5146]** which, according to the *Strong's* definition means *"a thistle, a prickly wild plant, hurtful to other plants."*[2]

What caught my attention right away with this definition is that a thistle is harmful to other plants. Thistles will damage any growth that you may have as a result of the seed of the Word being planted in your heart.

**"Tribolos"** is a combination of the words **"treis" [G5140 – three]**[3] and **"belos" [G956 – missile, dart, arrow]**.[4] When you research further into the root of "belos," you find that it is derived from the primary word **"ballo" [G906]**.[5]

According to *Strong's Concordance*, the primary definition of **"ballo"** is *"to throw or let go of a thing without caring where it falls."* I believe that this has become the standard in the modern day prophetic movement. With the way that prophetic words are spoken, prophetic ministers are trained and prophetic ministry is executed, the evidence of thistles is there - in abundance. Perhaps it has something to do with the *"three arrows/darts"* in the main definition? I'm not sure.

Let's discuss the thistle's "partner in crime" - the thorn - this is where things get deeper.

## THORNS CHOKE THE WORD

The "Parable of the Sower" **(see Mark 4:1-20)** is a very important parable to understand. Yeshua Himself said that if you can't understand this parable, then you won't be able to understand *any* of His parables! This includes parables about the End Times, the Kingdom of Heaven, etc.!

> **Mark 4:13**
> *And He said to them, "Do you not understand this parable? How then will you understand all the parables?"*

If the fruit of false prophets is associated with thorns and thistles, then the primary consequence of listening to them, and partaking of their teaching/prophecy/ministry, will be the choking of God's Word in your life, and **YOU WILL YIELD NO CROP**. We see this stated in the "Parable of the Sower."

> **Mark 4:7**
> *And some seed fell among thorns; and the thorns grew up and choked it, and it yielded no crop.* **(Also see Matthew 13:7 and Luke 8:7.)**

We know that the seed is the Word of God **(Mark 4:14)**. The seed of the fruit of the false prophet, when it enters the soil of your heart, *"chokes"* the seed of the Word, leaving you distracted, confused and unfruitful.

*So, how does the fruit of a false prophet choke the Word of God in your life?* Let's look at this key verse first:

> **Mark 4:18-19**
> *Now these are the ones sown among thorns; they are the ones who hear the word, and the cares of this world, the deceitfulness of riches, and the desires for other things entering in choke the word, and it becomes unfruitful.*
> **(also see Matthew 13:22, Luke 8:14)**

The false prophet will shift your focus away from hearing the pure Word of God through their false teachings and prophecies. Look at (or listen to) any of the prophecies from today's big name prophets and you will find the focus shifted from the Word of God to any of the following distractions.

## THE CARES OF THIS WORLD

When we think of *"the cares of this world,"* we usually think of worries, troubles and hardships that could distract us from our focus on the Word. I don't necessarily think this is a *wrong* way to view this portion of Scripture, but I do think that it is a very *narrow* view.

Let's look a little more closely and try to get a more complete picture of what Yeshua was trying to say.

How would the modern day false prophets choke the Word by using *"the cares of this world,"* as they are defined above? At first glance, with all the focus on creativity, feathers, gold dust and angels, it hardly seems a close match.

I was trying to find a good way to answer this question when I stumbled upon the following quote from a "word" the Elijah List put out in 2014. I have to say, the timing was perfect!

> *When God begins to speak of the future ... that is, when God prophesies to us, the devil is right there trying to give us "his own prophecies". The devil's prophecies are always a bold "in-your-face lie". The devil attempts to convince us that God is telling us dreadful things await us.*[6]

This perfectly demonstrates how a false prophet (and a false prophecy) will use the *"cares of this world"* to shift your focus away from the Word - by assuring you that God would NEVER say anything negative to you. In fact, the false prophet assures you that any "negative" you hear must be from the devil!!

*What does that have to do with the "cares of this life?"* I'll tell you.

This flies in the face of Scripture that says people WILL experience tribulation in the End Times, and that there ARE consequences of sin (both national and individual). When you constantly read false prophecies like this, you will grow accustomed to tuning out the Holy Spirit's voice when He convicts you of sin **(John 16:8)** and warns you of things to come on this earth.

You will even attribute it to the devil.

After all, the false prophet's reassuring message (*"Hey, everything is gonna be alright! Be at peace! God has nothing but GOOD things for you!"*) is so much easier to swallow!

But Jeremiah, a true prophet, says:

### Jeremiah 6:13-14

*Because from the least of them even to the greatest of them, everyone is given to covetousness; and from the prophet even to the priest, everyone deals falsely. <u>They have also healed the hurt of My people slightly, saying, "Peace, peace!" when there is no peace</u>.*

The false prophets of Jeremiah's day would always preach peace instead of repentance. Obviously, not much has changed. Steve Shultz even supports this false message in his intro to the article:

> *In this word from the Lord, Sandie (Freed) speaks of the wonderful things God has planned and then she gives a warning about a lying spirit that is called 'A foreboding spirit.' This is that same spirit from the devil with a special mission – to lie and bring fear about the future. <u>Ignore any spirit or flooding of thoughts that suggests God is not bringing good to His people in this 2014 year</u>.*[7]

Can you see the obfuscation and outright lies that are being promoted here? In order to steer you away from truth of the Word, you are being told to ignore anything that contradicts their "Word of the Day" because, according to the false prophet, it's either "fear" or "a lie."

### Lamentations 2:14

<u>*Your prophets have seen for you false and deceptive visions; they have not uncovered your iniquity*</u>*, to bring back your captives, but have envisioned for you <u>false prophecies and delusions</u>.*

### Jeremiah 14:13-14

*Then I said, "Ah, Lord GOD! <u>Behold, the prophets say</u>*

*to them, 'You shall not see the sword, nor shall you have famine, but I will give you assured peace in this place.'"*

*And the LORD said to me, "The prophets prophesy lies in My name. I have not sent them, commanded them, nor spoken to them; they prophesy to you a false vision, divination, a worthless thing, and the deceit of their heart."*

Rather than uncover your iniquity, a false prophet will prophesy to you false prophecies that comfort your flesh, but come straight out of the pit. One of these delusions is that God's people will have nothing but good, nothing but peace and safety!

Tell that to Peter, Paul, and John. Tell that to the believers in China and North Korea. They would laugh in your face... or weep at your gullibility.

## SO THEN WHAT IS THE ROLE OF A TRUE PROPHET?

### Jeremiah 23:21-22

*I have not sent these prophets, yet they ran. I have not spoken to them, yet they prophesied. But if they had stood in My counsel, and had caused My people to hear My words, then they would have turned them from their evil way and from the evil of their doings.*

It's really quite simple. The role of a true prophet is to cause you to hear God's words (see **Jeremiah 6:10, Acts 7:51** to read more on uncircumcised ears) and to turn you from your evil way (by following God's ways)... always. Any other focus is just "thorns and thistles."

Ahhhh, yes... let's get back to thorns and thistles.

*How does the message of the false prophet "choke the Word" like a thorn or thistle and cause you to be enslaved to "the cares of this world?"*

Understand this: <u>if you are not warned of any danger</u>, you will not prepare (spiritually or otherwise) for it. <u>If you are not admonished for your sin</u>, you will grow complacent and justify your own ways.

Just like the false prophets of old, the modern day false prophets will spoon feed you soft, comforting words, gradually lulling you to sleep. The flowery false prophecies that comfort your flesh leave you convinced that you are *"setting your mind on things above"* as you go about your daily routine.

But the truth is that you are consumed with the *"cares of this life,"* and are dictating to the Holy Spirit what He can and cannot say to you.

This is sin.

And the false prophets don't really care. The truth is, they would rather keep you happy and deluded than consecrated and righteous.

## WHAT ABOUT THE DECEITFULNESS OF RICHES?

Most of us who have been watching the prophetic and prosperity movements (both known for their false prophets) would think, "Oh, this is easy!" Along with the blatant charlatanism, the buying, selling and the resulting excess should make it obvious to everyone. The only ones who don't seem to notice are the ones benefiting from it.

So how do false prophets (and false prophecy) choke the Word in your life with the deceitfulness of riches?

Here is what happens. The false prophets will bring you a one-sided message, telling you that God wants to make you RICH and help you walk in ABUNDANCE. They will quote Scriptures such as:

### Philippians 4:19
*And my God shall supply all your need according to His riches in glory by Christ Jesus.*

### 2 Corinthians 9:8
*And God is able to make all grace abound toward you, that you, always having all sufficiency in all things, may have an abundance for every good work.*

...but will conveniently leave out verses like:

### Proverbs 11:4
*Riches do not profit in the day of wrath, but righteousness delivers from death.*

### Proverbs 11:28
*He who trusts in his riches will fall, but the righteous will flourish like foliage.*

### Proverbs 22:4
*By humility and the fear of the LORD are riches and honor and life.*

### Proverbs 23:5
*Will you set your eyes on that which is not? For riches certainly make themselves wings; they fly away like an eagle toward heaven.*

Now, in case I gave you the wrong impression, I'm not against walking in abundance and prosperity. There is nothing wrong with money and riches - it's the LOVE of money that is *"the root of all evil."* But unfortunately, we human beings are just too prone to this kind of covetousness.

Many will deny this - but many are liars!

Before you get offended, let me say that I fall into this category as well. The idea of never having to worry about finances is more than appealing to my flesh! Who in their right mind would NOT want to have the finances necessary to pay all their bills, plus get everything they ever wanted? It's just the way fallen man is wired.

Paul's letter to Timothy gives us some great instruction.

### 1 Timothy 6:9-12
*But those who desire to be rich fall into temptation and a snare, and into many foolish and harmful lusts which drown men in destruction and perdition. For the love of money is a root of all kinds of evil, for which some have strayed from the faith in their greediness, and pierced themselves through with many sorrows. But you, O man of God, flee these things and pursue righteousness, godliness, faith, love, patience, gentleness. Fight the good fight of faith, lay hold on eternal life, to which you were also called and have confessed the good confession in the presence of many witnesses.*

What we cannot deny, no matter how hard we try, is that we ARE covetous, and live among covetous people. We want *stuff* that has no eternal value and soft, fluffy, deceptive prophecies appeal to that want.

So what are we to do with verses like **Philippians 4:19** and **2 Corinthians 9:8** that, in theory, promise God's "endless supply?"

I think a great place to start would be to analyze the epistles in their entirety to determine exactly what kind of "need" Paul was addressing in its proper context. Next, we should take a good, hard look at our actual needs and separate them from what we think we need. Once we do this, I believe our view of these promises will change drastically.

Prophecies of abundance and provision without the consideration of maturity, obedience and humility are a breeding ground for misplaced hopes and desires, turning the hearers' ears and eyes away from the Word of God and robbing them of potential good fruit.

> **1 Timothy 6:17**
> *Command those who are rich in this present age not to be haughty, nor to trust in uncertain riches but in the living God, who gives us richly all things to enjoy.*

## THE DESIRES FOR OTHER THINGS

I realize that, at first glance, it may appear that I have blended *"the deceitfulness of riches"* and *"the desires for other things"* together in the last section. And it makes sense. "Riches" and a strong desire for "stuff' often go hand-in-hand. I believe Jesus already knew that when He spoke the "Parable of the Sower."

When I looked up *"other things"* in the Strong's Concordance, I found that the Greek word used here, **"loipos,"** does not refer to stuff like *"material possessions"* or *"women"* or other things that we usually associate with the word *"lust"* (although I'm sure it COULD include the items mentioned). No, the definition is much more general.

We see that **"loipos"** means *"the rest"* of something, or *"whatever is remaining."* If we fit this definition into the verse, it would read like this:

## Mark 4:18-19

*Now these are the ones sown among thorns; they are the ones who hear the word, and the cares of this world, the deceitfulness of riches, and the desires for <u>other things less important than the Word (Seed)</u> entering in choke the word, and it becomes unfruitful.*

This fruit is abundant in the prophetic movement. False prophets have an arsenal of diversionary goods to offer the hungry:

- *Beautiful music from skilled artists with melodic voices, using state-of-the-art instruments;*

- *Eloquent messages from a variety of personalities – from tattooed "free spirits," to kind and gentle old men;*

- *Daily "Words from God" that seem to promise the most wonderful rewards to* **EVERYONE** *who will grasp them "in faith";*

- *A virtual cornucopia of teaching materials – books, CDs, mp3s, DVDs, videos… all at your fingertips!*

- *Good, solid bible teaching? [sigh] Well… I guess you can't win them all…*

All of the above material is coupled with a focused emphasis on the following phenomena:

- *prophetic celebrity;*

- *healing, signs & wonders;*

- *angels;*

- *demons;*

- *unscriptural, purposely vague and inaccurate prophecy;*

- *gold dust, glory clouds & feathers;*

- *spiritual drunkenness and other spiritual "manifestations."*

With all of that **"loipos"** (residue, other things), the seed of the Word infrequently, if ever, gets planted. On the rare occasion a seed ever DOES implant itself, the **"loipos"** quickly smothers it, rendering the hearer *"unfruitful."*

## TYING IT ALL TOGETHER

In the last couple of chapters, we have discussed the fruit of false prophets and how they stand opposed to the fruit of the true prophet. Those who seek to partake in the ministry of a false prophet hear tales of (and are promised the rewards of) restoration and righteousness. What they are actually given is teaching and phenomena that may feel really good at first (I knew this feeling first-hand), but which actually robs them of the seed of the Word sown in their hearts, leaving them confused, barren and destitute.

To those who have devoted their lives to the dissemination of these "movements," I would say:

### Jeremiah 4:3b-4
*Break up your fallow ground, and and do not sow among thorns. Circumcise yourselves to the LORD, and take away the foreskins of your hearts, you men of Judah and inhabitants of Jerusalem, lest My fury come forth like fire, and burn so that no one can quench it, because of the evil of your doings.*

And keep in mind, thorns pierced the brow of our Messiah.

**Footnotes:**

[1] AnswersinGenesis.org: "Thorns and Thistles"
http://www.answersingenesis.org/articles/aid/v6/n1/thorns-thistles

[2] Blueletter Bible definition of the word "tribolos" [G5146]
https://www.blueletterbible.org/lang/lexicon/lexicon.cfm?strongs=G5146&t=KJV

[3] Blueletter Bible definition of the word "treis" [G5140]
https://www.blueletterbible.org/lang/lexicon/lexicon.cfm?strongs=G5140&t=KJV

[4] Blueletter Bible definition of the word "belos" [G956]
https://www.blueletterbible.org/lang/lexicon/lexicon.cfm?strongs=G956&t=KJV

[5] Blueletter Bible definition of the word "ballo" [G906]
https://www.blueletterbible.org/lang/lexicon/lexicon.cfm?strongs=G906&t=KJV

[6], [7] Elijah List: "Sandie Freed: Prophesy to the Dry Bones: 'The Time to Access the Unseen is NOW'"
http://www.elijahlist.com/words/display_word.html?ID=13027

[8] Blueletter Bible definition of the word "loipos" [G3062]
https://www.blueletterbible.org/lang/lexicon/lexicon.cfm?Strongs=G3062&t=KJV

# CLOSING THOUGHTS

Before I conclude this book, I want to address just a couple more issues that I believe will assist you in your discernment of false prophets and their tactics.

## THE PROPHETIC MOVEMENT IS BUILT ON CORRUPT DATA

Most companies that rely on computers to store customer and product information use a database. As a company grows, their database goes from a very small and simple source of information to a very complex and detailed program. During the creation and implementation of a database, it is imperative that the foundational structure of the database is absolutely perfect before you start adding information to it. If the database structure has undiscovered errors or disconnects, it can wreak havoc in the future.

If a company has used a faulty database for any length of time and an error is finally discovered, they will often look for some sort of "quick-fix" rather than rebuild the whole database, because the rebuild is usually expensive and inconvenient, but this is a HUGE mistake.

Once the issues are discovered, ignoring them (or postponing the rebuild for a later date) will only make things worse for the company. It is even possible that the data (or the database) can become so corrupted that the company will have to wipe the slate clean and start over. Nonetheless, many organizations still choose the quick-fix as a temporary solution. If they take this route, the chances are great that they will need to use another quick-fix in the future. I've even seen situations where a "quick-fix" was needed to repair a prior "quick-fix!"

Soon, the database begins to resemble Frankenstein's monster as they keep adding parts to a body of work that was flawed from its inception.

This analogy is very similar to what has happened with the "Prophetic" movement (and the "Word of Faith" movement, to some extent).

## PROPHETS AND PROPHECY ARE NOT WHAT YOU'VE BEEN TAUGHT

When you take scripturally incorrect definitions of terms like "prophet," "prophecy," and "prophesy" and mix them together with dispensational thinking, lies and demonically-inspired supernatural encounters, then present them to sincere people who desire an intimate relationship with God (albeit on their terms), you have a great recipe for a movement that will lead millions off the path of righteousness.

The founding fathers of this movement did not study the core terms mentioned above (prophet, prophecy, and prophesy). They merely read **1 Corinthians 14**, applied dispensational thinking (which basically pits the "Nice God" of the New Testament against the "Mean God" of the Old Testament, among other errors) and added in their own "divine revelation" based upon supernatural encounters of a questionable nature.

In doing all of the above, they have managed to completely twist, rearrange and transform the entire prophetic vocabulary in the Word of God.

- *They claim that the function of the prophet (and the nature of prophecy) has changed.*

- *They claim that now prophecy is only about encouragement – its sole purpose is to make you feel good about yourself.*

- *They claim that if conviction (they call it condemnation) comes as a result of a prophecy, then it is from the devil.*

- *Only seasoned prophets are allowed to bring any form of correction, and even then, it will happen only on a rare occasion.*

You will find this kind of perversion on prophetic web sites all over the Internet.

> *The very essence of the prophetic gift is more about encouragement than rebuke and causing others to see into their future. This promotes THANKSGIVING for what it's shown. Some exhortation or rebuke or warning is sometimes part of the prophetic but mostly, it's encouragement!* **– Steve Shultz, founder of the Elijah List** [1]

Such a philosophy is a load of… well, let's just say that it is "scripturally incorrect."

As I've stated before, **1 Corinthians 14** has been used (incorrectly) to justify all sorts of error in the prophetic movement. For a deeper understanding of this often misapplied chapter, check out my article *"New Testament Prophecy – Understanding 1 Corinthians 14,"* which I've included in this book as **Appendix C**.

From Genesis to Revelation, our God does not change, nor do His spokesmen, the Prophets. This is obvious to anyone who reads his bible. Do you remember the core message of the prophet?

*God is returning to set up His Kingdom! Repent from your wicked ways and return to His Ways! Obey His commands … all of them! If you do, GOOD things will happen! If you refuse, BAD things will happen!*

This is NOT what the false prophets preach, and this is NOT what the prophetic movement believes. They believe their own little man-made doctrines supersede what the Word of God says. And they call discernment ministries "Pharisees?"

Let's use our logic for a moment. If you base an entire "movement" on errant definitions of core terms (in this case "prophets" and "prophecy"), can you *ever* hope to walk in truth? Can you *ever* hope to walk in a true prophetic gifting?

No way. Not even close.

If you have an entire movement based on the wrong definition and application of core terms, you are already walking in deception from the start. Not to mention, you are opening wide the door for even greater deception to enter in.

The false prophets will try to add quick-fixes when the errors show themselves. Most of us who are familiar with the prophetic movement remember Bill Johnson and Rick Joyner's sketchy "restoration" of Todd Bentley. That, dear readers, was the mother of all quick-fixes.

Other false prophets try to ignore their errors entirely, hoping the after effects will go away or somehow right themselves without effort from them, and train their disciples to apply the same logic. How many times are we going to ignore Kim Clement's failed prophecies before we label him a false prophet?

This is all just a vain attempt to put lipstick on a pig, folks.

Like the faulty database mentioned earlier, the data is tainted and the delivery mechanisms are completely corrupted. This is not by accident, nor is it because we (or they) are "only human." This is due to a gross negligence toward the Word of God and a lack of willingness to face the truth by the false prophets and their followers.

In order to have a true "Prophetic Movement" inspired by the Word and Spirit of God, an entire restructure and rebuild needs to happen. And, I confess, I don't quite know how it is going to happen or what it's going to look like. All I know is that we need to 1) repent and 2) have the written Word of God as our foundation.

Let's do a little "side jump" to another topic before I close this book.

## THE TESTIMONY OF JESUS – THE SPIRIT OF PROPHECY

*"The testimony of Jesus is the spirit of prophecy"* is one of many tidbits of Scripture that has been tossed around by self-proclaimed prophets without the knowledge of what it really means. It leaves the unlearned with the inaccurate impression that, just as long as Jesus is being preached, the spirit of prophecy is present. Let's take a closer look at what the Scripture says about it.

> **Revelation 19:10**
> *And I fell at his feet to worship him. But he said to me, "See that you do not do that! I am your fellow servant, and of your brethren who have the testimony of Jesus. Worship God! <u>For the testimony of Jesus is the spirit of prophecy."</u>*

Usually when people read the above Scripture, they do not read it impartially; they read it through the lens they were taught to use. They don't ask themselves, *"What is the 'Testimony of Jesus?'"* In their minds, it is just a given that "The Testimony OF Jesus" is synonymous with "The Testimony ABOUT Jesus." This is wrong.

"The Testimony OF Jesus" is Jesus' testimony. It is *what* Jesus was saying *while* He testified on this earth. *What did Jesus testify?* The following Scripture gives us a good hint.

**John 7:7**
*The world cannot hate you, but it hates Me because I testify of it that its works are evil.*

Am I re-interpreting Scripture? No, I am not. I just refuse to spiritualize a verse when a much more practical explanation is available. The fact is that you and I can preach on Jesus all day long without the spirit of prophecy being present. Look at all the false prophets and the "Jesus" they preach.

- *Joel Osteen preaches a "feel good" Jesus;*

- *Kenneth Copeland preaches a "prosperity" Jesus;*

- *Chad Taylor preaches an "altruistic" Jesus;*

- *Brian "Hed" Welch preaches a "metalhead" Jesus;*

- *John Crowder preaches a "drunk/stoner" Jesus.*

These false prophets do not testify that the works of this world are evil, therefore they do not preach the *testimony* of Jesus. If they do not preach the testimony of Jesus, then the spirit of prophecy is not present.

True prophets like Isaiah, Jeremiah and Ezekiel had the same testimony as the ULTIMATE PROPHET, Jesus of Nazareth. They preached against the sins of the world AND the sins of the people who professed to belong to the God of Abraham, Isaac and Jacob.

The world and the religious posers hated them for it. But the Messiah obviously felt differently.

### Matthew 5:11-12
*Blessed are ye, when men shall revile you, and persecute you, and shall say all manner of evil against you falsely, for my sake. Rejoice, and be exceeding glad: for great is your reward in heaven: <u>for so persecuted they the prophets which were before you.</u>*

He also has something to say about the false prophets who preach *"another Jesus"* devoid of the spirit of prophecy.

### Luke 6:26
*Woe unto you, when all men shall speak well of you! <u>for so did their fathers to the false prophets.</u>*

You only need two or three witnesses to "establish" a false prophet.

So there you have it, ladies and gentlemen. Ten witnesses from Scripture describing false prophets from ancient times up to the present. Not much has changed.

Remember, the Word of God says:

### 2 Corinthians 13:1b
*In the mouth of two or three witnesses shall every word be established.*

I have given you ten witnesses, all backed up by an exhaustive amount Scripture and I'm sure there are plenty more witnesses that you can find if you search for them. I greatly encourage you to do so.

Now, go to the Elijah List links page[1] and apply these principles to the ministries that you see listed on that page.

- *Do they look like sheep?*

- *Do they draw a crowd?*

- *Do they speak presumptuously?*

- *Do they lead you away from God's Commands?*

- *Do they mimic the Spirit of God?*

- *Do they have false dreams and visions?*

- *Do they always have an "encouraging word?"*

- *Do they never seem to have an original thought?*

- *Do they perform miracles, signs and wonders?*

- *Do they produce bad fruit?*

Remember, you only need two or three witnesses to have a **biblically-certified false prophet**, but don't be surprised if you find that all TEN of these witnesses apply to some.

This quest to discern false prophets should not end with the Elijah List and their associated ministries. I want to encourage you to apply these criteria to ALL people who claim to operate prophetically.

Don't worry about offending the alleged "prophet" by doing this. If they are a true prophet of the Most High, they won't mind being held to the standard of His Word.

In fact, they'll welcome it.

I hope this book has blessed you.

Kevin Kleint

Web: http://www.honorofkings.org
Email: kevin@honorofkings.org

**Footnotes:**

[1] Elijah List links page:  http://www.elijahlist.com/links.html

# APPENDIX A:
# HOW TO TELL THE DIFFERENCE BETWEEN OLD TESTAMENT AND NEW TESTAMENT PROPHETS

When I left my job working for a well-known prophetic ministry, my understanding of prophecy and prophets was, at best, skewed. I knew that prophets and prophecy were real, and that the Bible talked about prophecy as one of the 5-fold ministries. Still, I knew that the fruits of our modern day "prophets" were NOT the fruits of righteousness and holiness, but greed, lust and licentiousness.

One day, I asked in desperation, *"God! Then how do I know a True Prophet and True Prophecy??"*

He replied, **"Kevin... READ THE PROPHETS!!"**

## THE END OF CONFUSION

Could it really be that simple? How is it that, in our quest to understand prophets and prophecy, we overlook about 1/3 (give or take) of the Bible? Did God know in advance that in the latter days, false prophecy would be so prevalent that His children would need a clear guide to discern between false prophecy and true prophecy?

I know this will upset those of you with dispensationalist training who believe that there is a difference between Old

Testament prophecy and New Testament prophecy, but the bottom line is that there isn't any difference.

You will not find anywhere in the Bible where God says... *"OK, now you prophets who were before Jesus, this is how you should prophesy. And you 5-fold ministry prophets... you prophesy this other way."*

It's simply not there. Not even in **1 Corinthians 14 (see Appendix C)**.

## EXPOSING SIN IS A PROPHET'S FORTE

God, speaking through the prophet Jeremiah, tells us a key characteristic of a true prophet:

> **Lamentations 2:14 AMP**
> *Your prophets have predicted for you falsehood and delusion and foolish things; <u>and they have not exposed your iniquity and guilt to avert your captivity [by causing you to repent]</u>. But they have divined and declared to you false and deceptive prophecies, worthless and misleading.*

True prophecy will expose sin for what it is - an abomination in the eyes of God. True prophecy will not play with sin. Sin separates God from His beloved children and He hates it.

Yes, He HATES sin!

But it is because of God's Love that He sends true prophets to His people to bring them to a place of repentance, so that the Divine relationship can be restored!

What is sin?

**1 John 3:4**
*Whoever commits sin also commits lawlessness, and sin is lawlessness.*

They Would Have Turned

Are you still not convinced? Let's try another verse:

**Jeremiah 23:21-22 AMP**
*I did not send these [false] prophets, yet they ran; I did not speak to them, yet they prophesied.  But if they had stood in My council, then they would have caused My people to hear My words, then they would have turned them [My people] from their evil way and from the evil of their doings.*

Now that's strange.  Where are their current instructions on "soaking" or how to have a "third heaven visitation?"  Could it be that we've missed the mark?  I'm not saying certain supernatural events will not take place in the life of a prophet, but those times are usually a result of consecration, service and sacrifice, not following the latest "5 Steps to a Heavenly Encounter."

## NEW TESTAMENT CONVICTION... BY ALL

Am I coming across as too legalistic?  Am I ignoring "grace?"  Doesn't the sacrifice of Jesus cover all those "doom and gloom" messages?    Let's look at prophecy in the New Testament for a minute:

**I Corinthians 14:23-25 NKJV**
*Therefore if the whole church comes together in one place, and all speak with tongues, and there come in [those who are] uninformed or unbelievers, will they not say that you are out of your mind?  But if all prophesy, and an unbeliever or an uninformed person comes in, he*

*is convinced by all, he is convicted by all. And thus the secrets of his heart are revealed; and so, falling down on [his] face, he will worship God and report that God is truly among you.*

Wow! That almost sounds like the Old Testament! Have the modern day prophets included this instruction in their user-friendly prophecy? No they have not.

I challenge you to take your understanding of what a modern day prophet is supposed to be and compare it to the Word of God.

God's Prophets paid a price. They didn't charge a fee.

# APPENDIX B:
# FALSE PROPHETS, FRUIT AND
# THE UNWITTING WOLF

When some of us picture a false prophet, we imagine an evil, sinister man (or woman) maliciously rubbing their hands together as they devise a wicked scheme to rob some poor, defenseless widow of her last few dollars. Others may picture a character from history, like Nostradamus, who grew quite popular for a time, but had a terrible track record.

According to Jesus' own words in **Matthew 7**, both of these stereotypes are very inaccurate.

As we look deeper into this passage, we will find that the false prophets at the End of the Age are people who probably have the best intentions. They may genuinely believe that they are doing God's will and have the signs and wonders to back up their claims! But when it's all said and done, the miraculous signs and wonders are not God's "Seal of Approval" on their lives and ministries.

Jesus will say *"I never knew you, depart from me."*

Let's take a closer look at **Matthew 7**, which will explain how to spot a wolf (and by extension, a false prophet).

## WOLVES AND COVETOUSNESS
### Matthew 7:15
*Beware of false prophets, who come to you in sheep's clothing, but inwardly they are ravenous wolves. You*

*will know them by their fruits. Do men gather grapes from thornbushes or figs from thistles? Even so, every good tree bears good fruit, but a bad tree bears bad fruit.*

Jesus starts off by comparing the false prophets to wolves. Metaphors tend to stay consistent throughout the Word. If you look up all of the instances of wolf or wolves in the Bible, most of the time you will see the characteristic of "hunger" brought to the forefront. In this passage, Jesus describes the false prophets as ravenous wolves.

A wolf's appetite will drive it to consume at all costs, especially when it is *ravenous*. Its desire is to feed off the flock's resources (meat) so it can satisfy its flesh or, in my redneck vernacular, to get "Stuff."

This is the definition of "Covetousness." Most of us have learned from our Sunday school teachers and pastors that to "covet" means to desire something that belongs to your neighbor. While this definition (derived from what we read in the 10th commandment – **Exodus 20:17**) is true in part, it is not complete.

To covet means to intensely desire something, and coveting has both good and bad sides.

The *good* side of coveting is that you could greatly desire the things of God. In fact, we are told to covet, or earnestly desire, spiritual gifts **(1 Corinthians 12:31)**.

The *bad* side of coveting is that you intensely desire things to satisfy your flesh and they don't just have to belong to your neighbor! It could be the latest DVD. It could be a new house. It could even be a new Bible! How many of you know that we in the Western church are definitely a covetous people?

I pray almost daily that covetousness (in a bad sense) will not be found in me, and that I will learn to be satisfied with what I have, because covetousness is one of two key characteristics found in false prophets.

## FALSE PROPHETS AND A SINLESS DISGUISE

End time false prophets (wolves) are covered in wool, which is symbolic of being sinless (according to **Isaiah 1:18**). Wool gives comfort to the one wearing it, whether it is the wolf, the sheep, or the people who wear the wool clothes. This appearance of holiness is a great disguise (and comfort) to the wolf, because if the flock is continually deceived, the wolf can continue to satisfy its ravenous hunger.

At this point, it would be really easy to hate the wolf, but you have to understand - it's a wolf's instinct to satisfy its hunger (desire) at all costs. In fact, it feels no remorse, no guilt and no condemnation for its actions.

A wolf only does what it knows to do.

In the same manner, a false prophet is only performing the way he/she knows how. In fact, a false prophet will actually think that he/she is doing the will of God! False prophets are deceived into thinking that they are obeying the Master, when actually they are absolutely driven to take from the flock... all the while hiding behind their wool (holiness).

## FRUIT OF THE FALSE PROPHETS

### Matthew 7:16-17

*You will know them by their fruits. Do men gather grapes from thornbushes or figs from thistles? Even so, every good tree bears good fruit, but a bad tree bears bad fruit.*

Here's something that we need to understand: Jesus didn't say that we would notice the false prophets by their teaching or by their prophecy. A false prophet will say things that are scriptural - or almost scriptural.

It's the **FRUIT** of the prophet that determines whether he/she is false or true. What kind of fruit should we look for? Most would immediately say *"the Fruit of the Spirit"* and they wouldn't be wrong to do so.

We should absolutely look for the Fruit of the Spirit operating in a prophet's life, but we also need to face the fact that this kind of fruit can be faked. It's very easy for a prophet to act one way in public but another way behind closed doors. To simply ignore this truth "in the name of love" is to ignore Christ's command to be *"wise as serpents"* **(Matthew 10:16)**.

## FALSE PROPHETS AND FAMILY

In addition to looking for the Fruit of the Spirit to determine whether we have a prophet or a wolf in our midst, we also need to look at what types of offspring (fruit – both spiritual and physical) is being produced by the prophet and his/her ministry.

- *Do their spouses and children seem happy and at peace?*

- *Do they live by a godly standard?*

- *Do the people who follow their ministry exhibit a godly standard?*

- *Do their prophecies come true, and do they bring people back to God in repentance?*

Using the points listed above (as well as this study in **Matthew 7**), you should be able to discern a false prophet fairly easy.

## MANY FALSE PROPHETS WILL COME

It is absolutely vital that we watch and judge prophets by their fruit. Jesus said in **Matthew 24:4b-5** *"Take heed that no one deceives you. For many will come in My name, saying, 'I am the Christ,' and will deceive many."*

Many want to interpret this verse to say that many will come claiming to be "the Christ" or "Jesus Christ" Himself. Aside from a very few exceptions, this is wrong! Look at the world around you! Have MANY come claiming to be Jesus? Aside from a few weirdos, not many. Have they deceived MANY? Nope.

But how many have come claiming that "Jesus is the Christ, the Anointed Son of God" - hundreds (maybe thousands)? How many have been deceived by their preaching - millions!

Jesus is saying "Take heed!" In other words, **"PAY ATTENTION – WATCH!"** Don't accept everyone who says they are a prophet (or pastor, or teacher, or apostle) with open arms!

## FALSE PROPHETS AND THE BAD SEED

There are many who want to reason it out and say, *"Well prophet 'so-and-so' started out genuine, but he was deceived by [enter any deception here] and now he's in error,"* but the Bible doesn't say that! The Bible says in the next verse:

### Matthew 7:18
*A good tree cannot bear bad fruit, nor can a bad tree bear good fruit.*

I understand that this is a very *absolute* statement. But the Word of God does not allow for the comfort of our flesh or our ever-changing human reasoning. In my flesh, I would say,

*"God, can't we just believe the best of all these ministries?"* Apparently not.

This verse leaves absolutely no wiggle room for the people who claim to be prophets... none!  They are either a bad seed or a good seed.  Let's continue.

## A FALSE PROPHET'S DESTINATION

### Matthew 7:19-20
*Every tree that does not bear good fruit is cut down and thrown into the fire. Therefore by their fruits you will know them.*

The end result for false prophets is not good. They're going to hell - plain and simple. The Word itself said that they (the false prophets – trees) will all be cut down and thrown into the fire.

**Side Note:** I know what some of you are thinking. *"Those are some big words for such a small guy!  He better hope that they don't come back to haunt him!"*

Let me tell you something - the fear of God has gripped me as I write this.  We are in a time where our fruit (good or bad) is being made manifest.  That fruit came from a planted seed. Just like the false prophets, I too am susceptible to manifesting bad fruit, so I am in no way better than anyone else.  But by recognizing the bad seed of covetousness (the lust for other things) in my life, I am able to uproot that seed and plant the seed of the Word in its place.

*It's healthy* to have the fear of God in this area. *We need* a greater fear of the Lord when it comes to ministry, anyhow. Jesus said that the road is narrow and few there are that find it.  I believe that verse; do you?

I'm also doing everything I can to understand the Word of God and take it at face value, and not go by the flawed teachings of man - which brings me to my next point.

## NOT EVERY PROPHET

### Matthew 7:21

*Not everyone who says to Me, "Lord, Lord," shall enter the kingdom of heaven, but he who does the will of My Father in heaven.*

Remember that the Word of God is exactly that - the Word of God! But the chapter breaks and the little section headers that divide up the Word are not. Many of our bibles treat the next few verses as a separate topic, but they are not.

**Verses 21-23** are certainly applicable to individual people, but in the context of these verses, Jesus was still talking about false prophets. Think about it for a moment: not everyone who names the name of Jesus is doing "miraculous signs and wonders," but miraculous signs and wonders are very abundant among the modern-day prophets.

### Matthew 7:22

*Many will say to Me in that day, "Lord, Lord, have we not prophesied in Your name, cast out demons in Your name, and done many wonders in Your name?"*

Can you hear the surprise in their voices? This is not the response of a wicked, malicious people! They are genuinely shocked that they are not allowed into the Kingdom. All the wonderful miracles in Jesus' name... all of the work done for the Kingdom culminates into one massive, righteous Rejection.

## NICE PEOPLE AND LAWLESSNESS

This should be an incredibly sobering moment in Scripture for all of us. Most of us are pretty nice people. Guess what? There are a lot of nice false prophets too!

Why are they rejected? Why would the Father turn them away?

> **Matthew 7:23**
> *And then I will declare to them, "I never knew you; depart from Me, you who practice lawlessness!"*

The Greek for "lawlessness" is anomia, which is a condition where you are without law.

Most of us have been taught that this is a general kind of lawlessness, as in being criminal in our actions, or indulging in a general sort of sin. But the root of the Word goes much deeper. The root is *anomos*, which is being in a state without GOD'S LAW.

I realize the last sentence may raise some red flags for some of you. And to try to list out (and explain) the handful of verses that most Christians use to support a law abolishing paradigm is well beyond the scope of this article. For now, we need to understand that, according to the words of Jesus, *"practicing lawlessness"* (practicing a lifestyle devoid of God's Law) will keep the false prophets (and you) out of the Kingdom.

## UNWITTING PARTICIPANTS

Jesus explicitly warned us to watch for false prophets and to avoid being deceived by their deceptive teaching. It's easy to spot the false prophets who are obviously way off the map. It's not so easy to spot the nice false prophet, who genuinely seems to be doing the work of the Kingdom. It's even more difficult when we realize that the fruit of the false prophet may be sprouting in our own lives.

Most of us have spent quite some time looking for false prophets among an obviously wicked group of people. But we need to comprehend that a modern day false prophet is not necessarily intentional in his or her deceit, but rather is an unwitting contributor to their own destruction. May we not be counted among their number.

# APPENDIX C:
# NEW TESTAMENT PROPHECY - UNDERSTANDING
# 1 CORINTHIANS 14

Prophecy is no joke. The words of a prophet are meant to birth repentance in the hearts of wicked nations, foretell the future and inspire hope in the hearts of the righteous followers of Yahweh. Unfortunately, we have strayed far from a scriptural definition of prophecy.

The following quote summarizes what most people believe about prophecy.

> *The very essence of the prophetic gift is more about encouragement than rebuke and causing others to see into their future. This promotes THANKSGIVING for what it's shown. Some exhortation or rebuke or warning is sometimes part of the prophetic but mostly, it's encouragement!* [1]

Those responsible for perpetuating this heretical mindset will have to answer to God when they stand before Him on that Great and Awesome Day, for leading an entire generation astray.

Right now, false prophets and teachers reason in their minds that there is a difference between the Old Testament Prophets and New Testament prophets, but there is no proof of that in His Word. In fact, the Bible says quite the opposite.

Before going forward, please read Appendix A: "How to Tell the Difference Between Old Testament and New Testament Prophets" It will provide more of a backdrop to what I am writing about in this article.

## THE FALSE PROPHET "PROOF TEXT"

Most of the modern day false prophets will parrot each other, using the following verse as their proof text for their definition of New Testament Prophecy.

### 1 Corinthians 14:3
*"But he who prophesies speaks edification and exhortation and comfort to men."*

If we were to isolate this Scripture, as many often do, and apply our current understanding of the words "edification," "exhortation" and "comfort," this would be great news! We would come to the simple conclusion that prophecy should be gentle and appealing to our emotions. However, if you take in the context of the surrounding Scripture AND the literal translation of the words, this assumption couldn't be further from the truth.

Let's dig deeper into Scripture and find out what the modern day false prophets refuse to acknowledge, and are terrified that you will find out.

## THE PURPOSE OF PROPHECY

### 1 Corinthians 14:1
*"Pursue love, and desire spiritual [gifts], but especially that you may prophesy."*

Here we see the importance of prophecy. We're supposed to pursue it above EVERY spiritual gift. This underscores how vital it is to get our understanding of prophecy right. Why is this so important? Because it has to do with the building up of the body of Christ - His church (ekklesia) - His called out ones. He wants us to succeed in His mission for us here on earth before He comes. We'll dig deeper into this as we progress further into this study.

### 1 Corinthians 14:3
*But he who prophesies speaks edification and exhortation and comfort to men.*

Let's not overlook this Scripture about prophecy, as it does offer a definition of what prophets are to accomplish in their prophesying to men. However, it is not meant to paint prophecy as a nice little spiritual gift that gives you a warm feeling all over your body when you hear it, as the false prophets would have you believe. <u>You will find that the false prophet's "proof text" will actually condemn the very ones who misapply it.</u>

What follows is a deeper look into the terms "edification," "exhortation" and "comfort," but before we go there, we need to understand that these terms cannot be correctly defined with our current Western mindset. Although God doesn't mind blessing His children with material "things" and letting us "feel" His love, His primary concern is our eternal destination, and whether or not we are walking toward that destination. As a result, our temporal comforts will always take a back seat to His eternal purpose for our lives.

## EDIFICATION (OIKODOME)

- *prophetic-prophet - (the act of) building, building up*

- *metaph. edifying, edification a. the act of one who promotes another's growth in Christian wisdom, piety, happiness, holiness*

- *a building (i.e. the thing built, edifice)*

When we see the *Strong's* definition **[oikodome - G3619]** of "edification," we see that it has to do with the act of "building up", strengthening, fortifying, and making stronger.[2]   The Old Testament Prophets tied the act of "prophesying" to building a wall.

### Ezekiel 13:4-5

*O Israel, your prophets are like foxes in the deserts. You have not gone up into the gaps to <u>build a wall</u> for the house of Israel to stand in battle on the day of the LORD.*

A prophet's role is to strengthen the believers so that when the day of battle comes (and it will come), they are able to stand. Now tell me what will strengthen a saint more - unscriptural prophecy that is easy on the ears and soothing to the emotions, or a prophecy that brings people to their knees in repentance? Read further and find out.

### Ezekiel 13:6-9

*They have envisioned futility and false divination, saying, "Thus says the LORD!" <u>But the LORD has not sent them; yet they hope that the word may be confirmed.</u> Have you not seen a futile vision, and have you not spoken false divination? You say, "The LORD says," but I have not spoken. Therefore thus says the Lord GOD: "Because you have spoken nonsense and envisioned lies, therefore I am indeed against you," says the Lord GOD. "My hand will be against the prophets who envision futility and who divine lies; <u>they shall not be in the assembly of My people, nor be written in the record of the house of Israel, nor shall they enter into the land of Israel.</u> Then you shall know that I am the Lord GOD."*

Why will all of the above come upon these false prophets?

### Ezekiel 13:10-12
*Because, indeed, because they have seduced My people, saying, "Peace!" when there is no peace - and <u>one builds a wall</u>, and <u>they plaster it with untempered mortar</u> - say to those who plaster it with untempered mortar, that it will fall. There will be flooding rain, and you, O great hailstones, shall fall; and a stormy wind shall tear it down. Surely, when the wall has fallen, will it not be said to you, 'Where is the mortar with which you plastered it?'"*

A false prophet will not warn you, he will seduce you. How will he seduce you? By saying "soft things" to you to lull you to sleep. The sad thing is the sheep want it that way.

### Isaiah 30:9-10
*That this is a rebellious people, Lying children, <u>Children who will not hear the law of the LORD</u>; Who say to the seers, "Do not see," And to the prophets, "Do not prophesy to us right things; <u>Speak to us smooth things, prophesy deceits</u>."*

Being disciplined as a child is almost NEVER pleasant, but it strengthens a person's character and shapes his/her personality. The same is true for prophecy. But the mature welcome rebuke.

### Proverbs 9:8
*Do not correct a scoffer, lest he hate you; Rebuke a wise man, and he will love you.*

## EXHORTATION (PARAKLESIS)
- *a calling near, summons, (esp. for help)*

- *importation, supplication, entreaty*

- *exhortation, admonition, encouragement*

- *consolation, comfort, solace; that which affords comfort or refreshment*

    o *thus of the Messianic salvation (so the Rabbis call the Messiah the consoler, the comforter)*

- *persuasive discourse, stirring address*

    o *instructive, admonitory, conciliatory, powerful hortatory discourse*

As you can see, "exhortation" **[paraklesis - G3874]** can include a combination of both "admonition" and "encouragement,"but I want to focus on the first definition - "a calling near."[3] This is the primary definition and, I believe, the intended one.

Look at how the prophets "exhorted" in the Old Testament (again, read Appendix A if you haven't, for my reasoning behind this). They were constantly calling Israel back to God, begging the nation to repent of their sins so that God's comfort could come.

Still not convinced? OK, fine, let's look at a New Testament exhortation from Peter.

> **Act 2:38-40**
> *Then Peter said to them, "Repent, and let every one of you be baptized in the name of Jesus Christ for the remission of sins; and you shall receive the gift of the Holy Spirit. For the promise is to you and to your children, and to all who are afar off, as many as the Lord our God will call." And with many other words he*

*testified and exhorted them, saying, "Be saved from this perverse generation."*

Do you see how exhortation did not change between the Old Testament and New Testament? Repentance and consecration (*"Be saved from this perverse generation."*) were vital components, just as they were in the Old Testament.

Most modern day prophets want to use the term "exhort" to mean *"spur one another on towards love and good deeds."* There's nothing wrong with "spurring one another on," but tell me, when you're exhorting in your prophesying, what is more important? To call someone nearer to God, or to preach "be nice?" Again, teaching each other to be nice isn't wrong, but that's a teacher's job; we're talking about prophesying.

## COMFORT (PARAMYTHIA)

- *any address, whether made for the purpose of persuading, or of arousing and stimulating, or of calming and*

- *consoling*

- *consolation, comfort* [4]

I can hear some of you saying "A-HA! We got him now!" Look back, I never said that comfort **[paramythia - G3889]** didn't have a part in prophesying. But again, we need to be using the Old Testament prophets for our model. God filled close to 1/3 of the Bible (give or take) with messages from the prophets, and it wasn't to show you how prophecy "used to be."

*When did the prophets speak of the comfort of God?*

It was always after Israel repented and returned to God! Make no mistake about it - God wants to show you favor (grace) and God wants to love on you, but it just won't happen without a consecration to His purposes.

## SO WHAT DOES PROPHECY LOOK LIKE?

With those 3 terms (edification, exhortation, comfort) firmly under our belts, we can see from the remainder of **1 Corinthians 14** how this fits together. Although it seems like exhortation and comfort are secondary in importance to edification (they are no longer mentioned in Paul's discourse on prophesying), you should be able to see how they all work together to build up the believers and keep them on the pathway to their eternal destination. Having said that, we need to see that edification is the focus for the rest of the chapter.

> ### 1 Corinthians 14:4-5
> *He who speaks in a tongue edifies himself, but he who prophesies edifies the church. I wish you all spoke with tongues, but even more that you prophesied; for he who prophesies is greater than he who speaks with tongues, unless indeed he interprets, that the church may receive edification.*

Here again, Paul talks about the importance of the edification of the church while prophesying. He also talks about it in **verse 12**.

> ### 1 Corinthians 14:12
> *Even so you, since you are zealous for spiritual gifts, let it be for the edification of the church that you seek to excel.*

Remember when I wrote earlier about prophecies causing repentance and how it was like building up the walls of Israel (God's people)? Are you still convinced that there is a difference between Old and New Testament prophets? Well, let's take a look at <u>yet another</u> New Testament example of biblical prophecy.

First, let me clarify something.

### 1 Corinthians 14:22
*Therefore tongues are for a sign, not to those who believe but to unbelievers; but prophesying is not for unbelievers but for those who believe.*

We can see here that prophecy is only for believers. Many in the prophetic movement want to go out and prophesy over unbelievers. According to this New Testament Scripture, you shouldn't do that. Perhaps it's because of the confusion surrounding terms used in the following verses.

### 1 Corinthians 14:24-25
*But if all prophesy, and an unbeliever* **[apistos - G571]** *or an uninformed person* **[idiotes - G2399]** *comes in, he is convinced by all, he is convicted by all. And thus the secrets of his heart are revealed; and so, falling down on [his] face, he will worship God and report that God is truly among you.*

The word "unbeliever" is the Greek word **"apistos,"** which actually means one who is unfaithful, faithless and not to be trusted.[5] "Unlearned", however, is the Greek word **"idiotes."**[6] This term needs to be taken in context, as there are a few definitions, but is most likely someone who may be a believer, but doesn't know much in regards to the faith.

These two people are prime candidates for prophecy as they, more than likely, need to be warned and have a lot of sin to repent of. **Verse 25** backs it up because we see that they are being convinced by all (more than one), they are being convicted by all, and their hearts are being revealed to all.

This flies in the face of the definition of modern-day prophets and modern-day prophecy, but it is the Word of God. I know this may be a wakeup call for some, and some of you may think it harsh, judgmental and heavy, but I'm not going to be found in opposition to God when He returns. We really need to get this right. Perhaps if we employ more scriptural edification, exhortation and comfort, the church can move forward and we can hasten the coming of our King.

**Footnotes:**

[1] ElijahList.com (11/24/2011) - "Steve Shultz: Thanksgiving at the White House(s)"
Link: http://www.elijahlist.com/words/display_word.html?ID=10477

[2] Blueletter Bible definition of the word "oikodome" [G3619]
https://www.blueletterbible.org/lang/lexicon/lexicon.cfm?Strongs=G3619&t=KJV

[3] Blueletter Bible definition of the word "paraklesis" [G3874]
https://www.blueletterbible.org/lang/lexicon/lexicon.cfm?Strongs=G3874&t=KJV

[4] Blueletter Bible definition of the word "paramythia" [G3889]
https://www.blueletterbible.org/lang/lexicon/lexicon.cfm?Strongs=G3889&t=KJV

[5] Blueletter Bible definition of the word "apistos" [G571]
https://www.blueletterbible.org/lang/lexicon/lexicon.cfm?Strongs=G571&t=KJV

[6] Blueletter Bible definition of the word "idiotes" [G2399]
https://www.blueletterbible.org/lang/lexicon/lexicon.cfm?Strongs=G2399&t=KJV

# Visit HonorOfKings.org!

Would you like to learn more about what the Word of God says without all the "fluff" of mainstream christianity? Check out HonorOfKings.org and subscribe to the email list!

*Because there's HONOR in searching out a matter ....*

Made in the USA
Middletown, DE
20 April 2017